FORGOTTEN FIELDS
OF AMERICA

World War II Bases and Training
THEN and NOW

by Lou Thole

PICTORIAL HISTORIES PUBLISHING CO., INC.
MISSOULA, MONTANA

LIBRARY OF CONGRESS
CATALOG CARD NO. 96-69800

ISBN 1-57510-010-X

First Printing   August 1996

TYPOGRAPHY Arrow Graphics
LAYOUT Stan Cohen
COVER GRAPHICS Mike Egeler

Pictorial Histories Publishing Company, Inc.
713 South Third Street West, Missoula, Montana 59801

INTRODUCTION

THIS BOOK tells the story of the build up of the U.S. Army Air Force just before and during WW II. Its focus is on the training bases, the men and women who served there, and what they did. The story is not intended to serve as a reference guide, filled with data. Rather, its intent is to relate from a human interest standpoint, one of America's greatest achievements as told through the eyes of those who were there. Surely, had we not built our Air Force as rapidly as we did, the outcome of World War II might have been quite different. It's really a story about what makes America great—individual freedom, courage, initiative, self sacrifice, and a belief in God.

Perhaps never again will Americans have the freedom to exercise their initiative and imagination as they did during WW II. Largely unencumbered by stifling governmental regulations and partisan politics, and united as never before, they went about building the foundation for the greatest aerial force in history. The results were magnificent and are a lasting testimonial to the American spirit.

The Battle of Britain was being waged over the skies of England in 1940 while America was slowly realizing that it might be involved in a war few wanted, but surely would come. For the most part America was still an isolationist nation. The war in Europe and the Far East was far away, few wanted any part of it. However, as time went by, it became more clear that, like it or not, we were going to be involved.

Thanks to the isolationist attitude of the Congress and the subsequent lack of funding for the military, America was unable to defend its interests in a world gone mad. So while the British were defending themselves, America began to prepare for war.

For perspective, just a year before the Battle of Britain, the U.S. Air Corps totaled about 25,000 men and had an annual capacity to produce five hundred pilots. A year later, when the Japanese struck at Pearl Harbor, the U.S. had just over one thousand aircraft "officially" suited for combat. Actually most of these planes were underpowered, poorly armed, and obsolete.

So while Britain was buying time, purchased with their lives and property, the U.S. prepared for war.

A high priority was given to the Air Corps. Virtually forgotten since the end of WW I, it had only seventeen air bases in 1939. It was through the courageous and farsighted wisdom of the newly appointed Chief of the U. S. Army Air Corps, Major General Henry H. Arnold that the process to build an Air Force was put into motion. In 1938 General Arnold realized, he had a monumental problem on his hands. There were only two training fields, Randolph and Kelly Fields and their capacity was about five hundred pilots per year. How do you increase the number of pilot trainees from five hundred per year to the thousands that would be needed in event of war?

Facilities simply did not exist. The lack of time to build the training fields, train the trainers, and produce the mechanics needed to maintain the planes required an entirely different approach to meet the need.

At this point, pilot training consisted of three distinct phases, Primary, Basic, and Advanced. Each course lasted ten weeks. This training time would vary throughout the war according to needs. For example, early in the war, some gunners went into combat never having fired a machine gun from an aircraft, and had no formal training on the subject. There was no formal gunner training program even by 1941.

General Arnold decided to enlist the aid of his civilian friends engaged in the private pilot training business to handle the then 12-week primary phase training. While the civilians were doing primary phase training, the Air Corps would focus time and effort on building facilities for the basic and advanced phases of the pilot training program. The nine original civilian schools contracted by the Air Corps for primary phase training would grow to over 60 and graduate more than 200,000 pilots.

The start-up of the primary schools was not as difficult as the more complex basic and advanced training fields. Primary schools could use grass fields, the planes were relatively simple in design, and easy to maintain. Housing facilities were spartan; students sometimes lived in tents while housing was being constructed.

The bases required for the follow-up phases of Basic and Advanced were much more complex. More important, with just a few exceptions, they did not exist. Each of these fields was a small self-contained town. They differed from each other according to their intended use, but in many ways were the same. They varied in size from about two thousand acres for a basic training base to over 65,000 acres for a bomb aimer training field. Population also varied. Many had over five thousand men and women living and working on the base either as trainees, trainers, or support personnel. Typically they were built from scratch on farm or vacant land and contained several hundred buildings of all descriptions. Of course, there were the runways, many 150 ft. wide and five to seven thousand feet long. Each field had hangars, generally about five, barracks, warehouses, complete hospitals (with operating suites), dental clinics, and maintenance shops. They contained libraries, social clubs, for officers and enlisted men, a jail (stockade), and stores to buy living necessities. Some had swimming pools, all had sports fields, and dining halls. Typically, they were built and ready for operation in about six months. The facilities vital to the training mission were constructed first, and that part took about six months. As time went by, the "luxuries," i.e., swimming pools, libraries, and officers clubs, were built as time and material allowed. Throughout the war they were constantly improved to make living more comfortable and the training more efficient.

The effort in time and material to build these bases was unprecedented, an undertaking never seen before in our history. At its peak in 1943, there were about 783 air fields, most of which were built during 1941 and 1942. Not all were complete installations. Some were subbases, and others were auxiliary landing strips. They would graduate, 224,331 pilots, over 46,000 navigators, more than 42,000 bombardiers, and 282,836 gunners. Construction of these fields during so brief a time span put an almost impossible demand on the need for building personnel and materials. All this was going on while the entire U.S. was shifting into high gear for the war effort. Factories had to be built and converted, and huge training facilities established for the Army, Navy and Marines. Meanwhile, able-bodied men were being taken out of the workforce in unprecedented numbers for military service.

Airfield construction workers often traveled from site to site moving on when their phase of the construction was completed. Typically, a field would require over 1,000 workers, some from the local area, and many from outside the town. The influx of

workers and their families presented tremendous problems, especially housing. Often, where the fields were built near small rural towns, the workers and assigned military personnel outnumbered the inhabitants of the town. Each town mainly had to cope on its own.

Most of these bases were designed as temporary training fields to be used only during the war. Construction was of wood, tar paper, and non-masonry siding. Concrete and steel were seldom used because of their need elsewhere.

Often, the military would arrive while the field was still under construction and training would begin, sometimes, while runway construction was going on. Frequently trainees and their trainers lived in tents and took their meals in the open, while barracks and mess halls were being completed.

By the end of 1943, the flood tide of new base construction was over. Plans were made to limit additional construction, and get rid of excess facilities. However some construction did go on, especially for those bases involved in the training of B-29 crews. Some excess bases were turned over to other services and others put on caretaker status. They were used for several purposes including prisoner of war camps, housing of foreign laborers, and agriculture operations.

With the end of the war, most of the training bases were gradually closed. Surplus material such as office furniture, office supplies, small hand tools, beds, mattresses, photo equipment, etc., was sold in small quantities. Other excess material was given away to schools or simply dumped into trenches and buried. Some equipment was transferred to other bases, or put into storage. Buildings were dismantled, and the lumber sold by the truckload for a dollar. Because of the desperate housing shortage following the war, many former barracks were converted into housing. At one field, the 80-acre building site containing 137 buildings was converted into a small town, renamed for a local public official, and used into the early fifties when it was finally torn down.

Many of these "temporary" fields and buildings are still in place, scattered across the United States. Occasionally, they are derelict and abandoned, the long concrete runways and remains of building foundations slowly being concealed by weeds and brush. Others have been converted to industrial parks, where the concrete runways have made excellent building foundations. A few still serve as active Air Force installations.

These fields, and the men and women who served

there, have passed into history. Most of the former training fields are quiet now, the roar of their engines long since replaced by the whisper of the wind and the rustling of leaves across silent runways. Walking across these deserted fields, you know something special happened here. As magnificent as it was, you pray it will never happen again.

Acknowledgments

I AM DEEPLY indebted to many people for the publication of this book. Without their help, it would not have happened. In a way, the book was a family adventure. My wife, Jane, contributed insight, ideas, and support. Much of the proofreading was done by our daughter Elizabeth. She also took pictures on one of my aerial jaunts to Freeman Field. They turned out well, especially in view of the fact that it was just her third flight in a single-engine airplane. All were flown by her father, a newly minted private pilot. Our younger son Chip, accompanied me to many of the "Forgotten Fields" and helped visualize how the field was through his ability to read the original construction plans. He was good company. David, our oldest son, provided a great deal of the inspiration. Much of the book was written as he was undergoing cadet training at the Air Force Academy. Finally, to my deceased sister, Elaine Schramm, who encouraged my writing, and was one of my greatest fans.

While writing the book, I was privileged to meet many wonderful people, some who played a major role in the history covered in this book. They gave freely of their time and experiences, and shared photos and memories with me. They include Ray Boudreaux, Tom Brewer, Dorothy and Jim Bunker, Virginia Brunner, Paul and Bel Cramer, Patricia Dunston, Mel Eisaman, Don Eret, Robert Fischer, Mel Gerhold, Stratton Hammon, Bob Ingmire, David Menard, Roger Myers, Walt Pierce, Jimmy Porter, Jim Ross, Wendell Ross, Robert Schirmer, Bob Schott, James Schmelzle, Dawn Seymour, Ed Shenk, Dave Timbers, and Donald Weckhorst.

A special debt of gratitude to Horace Dimond and Ray White, who both served in the United States Air Force during WW II. Their unique experiences and knowledge of this period of our country's history were invaluable contributions to the book.

Foreword

THIS BOOK TELLS the story of the expansion before and during World War II of the United States Army Air Forces. Its focus is on the training fields used to prepare the young men for aerial combat, and that's where I come in. I am a proud member of Class 40A, the first expansion flight class initiated by General "Hap" Arnold, Chief of the Army Air Corps—later changed to the Army Air Forces. This first class would graduate 226 second lieutenants, seventeen of whom later became generals. Twenty-eight lost their lives in combat. The class won seven Distinguished Service Crosses, one Navy Cross, 135 Distinguished Flying Crosses, and two British Flying Crosses. We were the first to hear the Air Corps song played for us at Randolph Field, Texas, in the summer of 1939 by Robert Crawford.

I first met Lou Thole after my flying class asked me to commission a memorial to Class 40A at the United States Air Force Museum in Dayton, Ohio. Lou had written an article about Baer Field, Fort Wayne, Indiana, and mentioned that the first landing at the field was made by a P-39 pilot. I recognized that this information was not accurate. Although a P-39 did make a landing before the field was dedicated, mine was made a few day earlier. It was made on the north-south taxiway during a high wind condition in a Stearman PT-17. I contacted Lou with the proper information, and later he wrote a sequel to the original story. Since then, we have worked and flown together on some of his pet projects until 1995 when he asked me to write the Foreword to his book. I was honored to have been asked to participate in his literary effort, and agreed to try. To be thrust into a job of letters with little or no experience is a nerve-wracking experience at best.

Class 40A began in the summer of 1939 and graduated at Kelley Field, Texas on March 23, 1940. Of course, everyone had his own idea of what part of the Air Corps he was desirous of joining, but recognized that the edicts out of Washington, D.C. would be the order of the day. Most assignments were accepted in good spirits and without major objection. So away we went to our first duty stations. One of my assignments was with the First Pursuit Group, Selfridge Field, Michigan. There, I was assigned to fly a P-35, one of the aircraft richly touted as the brainchild of Major Alexander D. Seversky, well known in aviation circles. It was indeed a thrill to fly this well known fighter and I did so with the appropriate gusto.

Later in May 1941, a call went out for volunteers to talk with members of the Curtiss Wright Corporation, which was recruiting fighter pilots for a specific job in the Orient to counteract the advance of the Japanese, still involved with the "Rape of Nanking." One of my classmates, Lieutenant Robert (Duke) Hedman and I arrived at the Booke Cadillac Hotel in downtown Detroit to meet with the representatives of the Curtiss Wright Company. When I was asked how much fighter time I had, my answer must have been totally dismaying to my interviewers, for my total fighter time was something in the neighborhood of 22 hours, although my total time was close to 1,200 hours in multi-engine craft. Of course, I was disqualified and returned to my base. Duke, however, became a valued member of the American Volunteer Group, ultimately known as the "Flying Tigers" in 1941. Hedman flew the early P-40 Curtiss fighter and became an Ace in his first air battle over Rangoon, Burma. He is credited with a total of nine enemy aircraft including six bombers and three fighters. After the war, Duke became Vice President of Flying Tiger Airlines, which operated worldwide for many years.

Some other well known members of Class 40A included General David Burchinal, whom I first met in July 1939. After graduation we separated, and he went on to become secretary to the Joint Chiefs of Staff. Later, after earning his fourth star, he was deputy commander of NATO. Another member of our class, General Tom McGehee, was given the task of building a site for electronic surveillance that was to be safe from nuclear attack. The center was located deep within a mountain near Colorado Springs, Colorado. Today it is known as Cheyenne Mountain, the headquarters for NORAD, the North American Air Defense Command. Colonel William Leverette's portrait hangs in the Art and Museum section of the Pentagon in Washington, D.C. After graduation he went on to become an instructor in air tactical warfare incorporating his own ideas of fighter tactics. He put this to good use while a squadron commander in North Africa early in WW II. In one air battle he shot down seven enemy aircraft over the island of Rhodes. He earned the Distinguished Service Cross, the Distinguished Flying Cross, and the

Air Medal with thirteen oak leaf clusters.

The "Forgotten Bases" Lou writes about were all constructed for the war effort, and although I did not know it at the time, I made a minor contribution to their establishment. During my early service at Selfridge Field, one day, without warning, the Commanding Officer of the 71st Pursuit Squadron told me to report to headquarters for a special assignment. I was immediately interviewed about my experience in photography, although I assured the command that I had no aerial photo experience. However, they decided that my experience could be qualifying—perhaps they had no other choice. I was relieved from assignment with the pursuit group and reassigned to headquarters for a special assignment in aerial photography. With charts and instructions on the conduct of an aerial survey, in addition to maps of several surrounding states, I was directed to make aerial photos of several of the potential airfields in Ohio, Michigan, Illinois, and Pennsylvania. Provided with a North American AT-6 aircraft, an enlisted photographer with both K-19 and K-21 aerial cameras, and a carte blanche as to a specific reporting headquarters, I set off on my mission. These photos were to provide the data for possible expansion into war-time training bases. The reason for my mission was communicated to me only later after I had photographed several states. My photo mission lasted until approximately September 1941 when I was relieved of the assignment and transferred to a newly constructed military airfield called Baer Field near Fort Wayne, Indiana. This installation would have considerable impact on training Army Air Corps personnel. Once there, I would take on a new duty and was soon engulfed in setting up an engineering operation to service the transient as well as the locally based aircraft. I manned this position until just after the Pearl Harbor attack on December 7, 1941. Then I was assigned to an air base unit and left for overseas.

I am pleased that Lou began writing his stories while there still existed people who remembered the many airfields that provided the training facilities for the pilots, navigators, and bombardiers of World War II. Some of these stories will be told and retold for many generations, depicting the epics of bravery and self sacrifice from those who trained long and hard at the airfields that carried a nation to victory fifty years ago.

HORACE E. DIMOND, *Major USAF Ret.*
Springdale, Ohio
1995

Contents

. . .

BUILDING AN AIRFIELD

Atterbury Army Air Field

THE RAPID expansion of the Army Air Corps was well underway by the 1941 fiscal year; however, with the fall of France, the need for a stronger defense became even more apparent. As a result, Congress passed a succession of spending bills that ultimately would provide for the annual training of 70,000 pilots.

To speed building of the needed bases, the responsibility for their construction was moved from the Quartermaster Corps (already overburdened with other military needs) to the Corps of Engineers. Procedures to locate the bases, approve the sites, and authorize construction became less cumbersome, all in the interest of building the bases as quickly as possible. A sense of urgency eliminated much of the red tape associated with government projects; we needed the bases now.

There was no specific master plan for the arrangement of the expansion training bases, just guidelines. While many bases had similarities, most were unique, and were built according to the mission of the base. However, there were exceptions. For example, the pilot basic training base at Coffeyville, Kansas, was duplicated very closely by another base just a few miles down the road at Independence, Kansas.

Structures were another story. They were generally the same in terms of construction and design. For example, there was a standard barracks type building, hangar, post office, mess hall, hospital, chapel, etc. This speeded construction and helped improve quality control. However, this was subject to local needs. For example, in the Northeast, a base used structures called "hutments" to house personnel instead of the barracks type buildings found on many bases. Construction material also varied, some bases used prefabricated siding for wood, and others used cinder blocks for some buildings.

The building idea was designed around the concept of "Spartan" simplicity. General Arnold noted in January 1942 that "all frills and nonessential items would be eliminated and only the bare essentials would be approved." What this meant was buildings were to be of a temporary type built of wood and tar paper. Airfield construction during this period employed three types of building construction, Permanent, Mobilization, and Theater of Operations. Permanent buildings were constructed of brick and mortar for those bases intended to be used for an extended time. As a result, there were few buildings of this type on the temporary bases built for air crew training. The Mobilization type of building was of wood frame construction, often two stories, and was generally heated centrally by a coal burning stove with a duct system to spread the heat throughout the building. The more common type of building constructed was the Theater of Operations. This building was little more than a tarpaper shack set on concrete blocks, or a cement slab, and heated by a coal burning stove located in the middle of the building. These buildings were bitterly cold in the winter, and offered little protection from the heat and dust of summer. They were cheap, easy to build, and went up fast. It was estimated they could be built in one-sixth the time of the Mobilization type buildings, and were about one-fourth the cost. Probably the most enduring structures of the training bases were the hangars, typically built of wood with some steel and/or concrete. Some bases, where bomb aimers were trained, were required to maintain a secure building to store the top secret Norden bomb sight. Typically, a vault-like structure to house the bomb sight, was built within the standard temporary building. The vaults were made of steel reinforced concrete, with heavy steel doors. As a result, many of these safe-like structures are still standing, though the buildings that housed them have long since vanished.

Atterbury Army Air Field is a good example of the construction process that went on during the rapid build up of the Army Air Forces in 1941, '42 and '43. During this period, frantic construction was going on all over the United States. Plants were built or converted for war time production, ship yards were constructed, as were major training facilities for Infantry, Marine, and Navy personnel. Also, there

Aerial view of the field, circa 1942. The runways are complete and the building area is under construction. The major part of the construction was completed by December 1942. USAF

Columbus Municipal Airport as it is today. ROSS

was a need for technical schools to instruct mechanics and specialists in radio/electronic repair, schools for instructors, and major facilities for the production of ammunition. As a result, materials and people were at a premium.

Atterbury Army Air Field was located about 3 miles north of Columbus, Indiana, just east of U.S. route 31, about 35 miles south of Indianapolis. Within a 30-mile radius, were two other major military installations, Camp Atterbury, a 40,000-acre Infantry training camp with 1,780 buildings, and Freeman Field, an advanced twin-engine training field, with over 400 buildings. All were being built during 1942.

During this time, Mr. Stratton Hammon, a highly successful architect for twenty-two years and the owner of his own firm for thirteen years, took and passed the Army physical. He later received a letter appointing him a captain in the Corps of Engineers with orders to report to the Louisville District office. In his book, *The Impact of World War II On A Citizen Solider*, Stratton wrote, "From the Corps of Engineers' point of view, I was, perhaps the greenest officer ever to report for duty. At least I felt that way. One of the first things that struck me was that everything—tables, chairs, boxes, whatever, was stamped 'USED'. Since they were obviously not new and were apparently used, it puzzled me why they had to be labeled in that manner. It was several days before I realized that this stood for 'U.S. Engineer Department.'"

Stratton spent several months in the office, and later, on an airfield construction project learning about the duties of an area engineer and a little about the Army way of doing things. He also had to master the engineering knowledge necessary to build an airfield. A few months later, he was called back into the Louisville District office and appointed area engineer, contracting officer, and commanding officer of an Army airfield to be built 35 miles south of Indianapolis in Columbus, Indiana. This was on July 29, 1942, and he was given five months to build the field. Stratton's spending limit was one million dollars (in 1942 dollars) per day, and with a phone call to his boss, could have the limit increased to 10 million dollars per day. In today's dollars that would be about 130 million.

Hammon's only equipment was a small truck, some office supplies, and a map to Columbus. He drove there, borrowed a secretary and a jeep from his friend who was building camp Atterbury, and set plans to build the field. His first step was to visit the local Chamber of Commerce to ask for office space and clerical help. The Chamber of Commerce knew nothing of the project; however, they were most helpful. At this time, the farmers living on the land did not know that they would soon have to leave. Some farms had been in the same family for generations as land grants since the Revolutionary War. Prior to Stratton being ordered to build the field, the Corps of Engineers Real Estate section surveyed the field and declared it suitable to build a training field. One of the earliest mentions of the field occurred in the August 5, 1942, edition of the *Columbus Herald*. The article reported "an Army base to be built one mile north of town."

Stratton's initial responsibility was to find an architect/engineering firm who in turn would hire a contractor to build the field. The contractor would submit a bid based upon the architect/engineering firm's plans and specifications. This typically took about ten days. Stratton's job was then to insure quality control, meet construction time tables, handle labor issues, take care of local concerns, and make certain construction materials arrived on time and were of sufficient quality and quantity. He was also the official representative for the military and, as such, had considerable power to insure the field was finished within the required time.

One of the more difficult parts of the field's construction were the runways. They had to be poured to exacting specifications, and with the approaching winter, needed to be completed quickly. Adding to the normal difficulty of runway construction was the lack of material. Everyone was pushing suppliers to the limit for material. Before the start of runway construction, Stratton called a friend in Indianapolis with whom he had done business for years, and requested 10 rail cars of cement and 55 carloads of aggregates (sand and gravel) per day. The friend said unfortunately there simply was not that kind of quantity available, and in any case, Stratton was number 40 on the list to receive the material. Obviously, there wasn't time to wait, so Stratton called his colonel in Louisville to tell him of the problem and ask if there were anything Stratton could do. His colonel pointed out that Stratton had the power of eminent domain and that he should simply take control of the company. So he did. Stratton marched in with two of his officers, announced he was taking control of his friend's company, and moved his name to first on the list. He got his material on time.

. . .

View of the airfield site before the start of construction, August 1942. The Pennsylvania Railroad tracks are on the left edge of the picture. Later a spur was built from this line to the base. HAMMON, CORPS OF ENGINEERS

Another view of the farm land before construction. At the time, there were 12 farms on the airfield's location, August 1942. HAMMON, CORPS OF ENGINEERS

. . .

Preparation of ground before runway construction, August or September 1942. HAMMON, CORPS OF ENGINEERS

Early construction of the Northwest-Southeast runway, September 1942. The runway is still used today. HAMMON, CORPS OF ENGINEERS

. . .

Examples of "Theater of Operations" type construction. The buildings were of woodframe construction with exterior walls of prefabricated composite material. The buildings had no toilet or bathing facilities and were built with a life expectancy of five years. Exterior siding often varied from base to base depending upon availability of materials. The buildings were under construction at Bowman Field, Kentucky in February 1943.

HAMMON, CORPS OF ENGINEERS

Examples of the "Mobilization" type structure. Mobilization type buildings were built on some larger training bases and were much more comfortable. Shown are a barracks, parachute loft, and chapel *(next page)*. These pictures were taken at Bowman Field, Louisville, Kentucky while it was under construction in 1942 and 1943.

HAMMON, CORPS OF ENGINEERS

. . .

Before Atterbury was built, it was simply open farm land with a rudimentary road system. Roads had to be built and material found to build a rail siding onto the field. Stratton called the Pennsylvania Railroad requesting they build a rail spur onto his field. They did not have the rails and again many construction projects were already waiting for a rail spur. Hearing of the necessary rails in an abandoned nearby coal mine, he sent a crew to get the rails. Unfortunately, someone had already beat him to it. Here, Captain Hammon broke the chain of command and made a direct call to Mr. Donald Nelson, head of the War Production Board. Two days later, the Pennsylvania Railroad was building the spur onto his field.

Another time, he needed fire plugs, and was unable to get them because of the shortage. However, knowing where they were stored, he sent a truck over at night, broke through the fence of the storage yard, and took the necessary plugs. All was forgiven when he paid the bill. Someone else had to wait to get their fire plugs.

Winter was fast approaching, and the runways had to be put down if there was to be any hope of opening the field on time. Cold weather would complicate the process. Normally, concrete was not poured in freezing weather, but the option to wait for spring did not exist. It became necessary to pour concrete twenty-four hours a day, seven days a week, but he got it done. Later, when talking about this with his colonel, Stratton asked, "Why did you assign the area engineers who had been architects to engineering projects, and the engineers from civilian life to architectural jobs?" He answered, "You all knew how

to build, but by assigning you projects outside your disciplines, you did not know the jobs I gave you were impossible, so you did them." So the runways were put down, and it must have been done well, because they are still there 53 years later.

Another challenge to overcome was an incredible labor shortage. Laborers from all over the country came into Indiana to work on building projects. Often, laborers had to work long hours in poor weather, and at a pay rate many felt should be higher. Strikes and work stoppages were not uncommon, and union problems existed from time to time. Workers frequently left for better paying jobs. A local Columbus paper, *The Evening Republican*, ran a head-line story about construction worker problems at nearby Camp Atterbury. The story reported that a carpenter shortage was caused by wage conflicts, poor transportation facilities, and the possibility of new plant construction in Indianapolis. Often, union officials would visit the construction site, and provoke work slowdowns. One particularly trouble-some union representative was causing a problem for one of Captain Hammon's foreman. So the fore-man asked Stratton what he should do. Stratton said to lock him up, meaning just detain him for a few hours. Stratton went about his business and forgot the incident. About ten days later, Captain Hammon's boss called and asked if he were holding a civilian, Stratton replied, "Let me check." He did, and found the union official had been held in the field's jail for the past ten days. The foreman obviously mis-understood Stratton's suggestion. It turned out well however, because the official had been a fireman and was currently out of that job. So Captain Hammon

One of the remaining
hangars, this was Bldg. 111.
Picture taken in 1995. THOLE

This was the maintenance
shop during WWII. It con-
tained the carpenter shop,
propeller shop, battery
shop, machine shop, the
maintenance control sec-
tion, the tin shop, and a
forge and welding shop.
THOLE

Another view of the hangar
and Maintenance building
as they were in 1995. THOLE

Several views of former enlisted men's barracks taken in 1995. These are good examples of "Theater of Operations" type construction. Built to last five years, some are still in use today by small business firms. All are scheduled to be torn down. THOLE

appointed him the field's fire chief. Often union organizers would pose as workmen to gain entrance into the field. Since they appeared to be in excellent physical condition, Stratton asked the draft board in Indianapolis why these young men were not fit for military service. Soon these men began to disappear, and when the word got around, Stratton's union troubles were, for the most part, over.

The field was finished on time, and turned over to the Army Air Corps on Dec. 31, 1942. It covered over 2,000 acres and, when opened, had about 139 buildings. Until May 1944, there was no significant, long-term use of the field. Units were briefly assigned, spent just enough time to organize, and do some training, then were transferred. These units included a reconnaissance group, and some medium bombardment groups. However, in 1944, this changed when Atterbury was transferred from the 3rd Air Force to the First Troop Carrier Command of the 1st Air Force.

During 1944, the Army was involved in a massive training program for glider pilots. Many fields in Indiana participated, including Atterbury. Almost 18,000 men were enlisted in the glider program, but only about 5,000 received their pilot wings. There were simply more trainees than the anticipated glider building program could provide for. Glider pilot trainees came from many sources including instructors at civilian flying schools, washouts from the Air Corps Cadet programs, and men from other military units. Typically, they would solo in a small single engine plane, and then report for glider training with about 10 hours on the single engine ship. At this time, glider training was about 50 hours. After graduation, the trainees were commissioned as flight officers. Merton Wheeler was a C-47 pilot stationed at George Field near Lawrenceville, Illinois, and remembers it well. There wasn't room at Atterbury Field for the C-47 tow planes and the gliders, so the C-47s were kept at George Field. There were about 150 C-47s and C-46s at George Field and about 30 CG-4A gliders at Atterbury. Since George Field was a short flying time from Atterbury, the arrangement worked well. Merton recalls flying in all kinds of weather, and some days when even "the ducks were walking." His only close call came during a particularly overcast day with extremely poor visibility. While towing gliders in formation, he heard a thud in his ship and it shook slightly. Since he saw nothing and the C-47 flew well, he continued with his training flight. After landing, while checking his plane, he noticed the astrodome had been smashed. To this day, he doesn't know what hit him, but assumes it was a glider being towed by a different C-47. After that incident, Merton was more careful to make sure his parachute was in its proper place.

There were no fatalities during this period, but there were many landings in the fields around Atterbury. Getting the gliders back was a problem, because disassembling them to be trucked back was difficult and time consuming. As a result, a system was used that literally snatched the glider from the field into the air to be flown back to the air base. Here's how it worked. A tow line about 300 feet long was attached to the nose of the glider and laid out in front. It was then connected to a line stretched between two 12-foot poles. A specially equipped C-47 with a hook caught the tow line and "snatched" the glider into the air. Normally pilots flying from Stout Field in Indianapolis were called in to fly these missions.

Atterbury Army Air Field played an important role in the training of the first Black bomb group ever activated. In late 1944 and early 1945, when Atterbury had reached its peak personnel load of 1,400 officers and enlisted men assigned for training, the field was the training site for the 618th and 619th Bomb Squadrons of the 477th Bombardment Group (M). Although the group was assigned to Godman Field, Kentucky, the two squadrons were to train at Atterbury for four months, after which they were to return to Godman and be replaced by the other two squadrons. The training was First Phase (Pre-Crew) flying. Permanent crews had not been assigned primarily because of a lack of trained gunners. Gunnery training was taken elsewhere in places like Buckingham Army Air Field near Ft. Myers, Florida, and Yuma Army Air Field, Yuma, Arizona. Besides flying training, instruction was also given in armament, bombsight, chemical warfare, communications, and navigation. In early January, several groups of trainees had returned from their aerial gunnery training, so radio/gunners, engineer/gunners, and armorer/gunners were now available. Second phase (Crew Training) started; however, within a few months all 477th training activity at Atterbury was transferred to other fields.

In early 1944, the War Department began the expansion of the existing hospital at nearby Camp Atterbury (an infantry training center). Eventually, it became one of the largest military hospitals in the United States. Atterbury Army Air Base was used to fly in wounded from Europe and Asia, who would then be transferred to the hospital. Less than one

Atterbury Army Air Field headquarters building as it was in 1986. It has since been removed for new construction. THOLE

hour elapsed from the time the wounded landed at Atterbury Air Field to their admission to Wakeman General. The airbase was twelve miles away. Some men were flown from France, but most were from England. Their first stop was at Mitchel Field, New York, and from there it took about four and a half hours to fly to Atterbury Army Air Base. The hospital was named Wakeman General Hospital, and when finished, was enormous. It covered 80 acres and had a total of 68 buildings. Most buildings were two stories high, many made of concrete block. Others were air-conditioned and most were interconnected. The hospital specialized in neurosurgery, plastic surgery, and treatment of orthopedic cases. Some of the best specialists in the world worked there, and the hospital achieved nationwide recognition for its pioneering work in plastic surgery. The first casualties arrived from overseas in April 1944, and they would be followed by 86,500 more before the hospital closed in December 1946.

In February 1945, there were 1,840 military personnel and 600 civilians working at Wakeman General Hospital. During this period, Atterbury Air Force Base reached its peak World War II activity with glider training and hospital planes landing throughout the day. This continued through V-J day when glider training was generally phased out. Hospital planes continued to use the field until Wakeman closed. Today, the chapel, administration building, doctors' and nurses' quarters, and the indoor swimming pool still remain. Some are in use by the Job Corps.

The control tower as it was in 1945. USAF

. . .

After WW II, Atterbury Army Air Field was deactivated. However, it was used from time to time to train pilots. Carl Lawhorn was a pilot with the 167th Fighter Squadron, West Virginia National Guard, and remembers flying F-51s there in the summer of 1948 for his two weeks of active duty training. Carl recalls opening the barracks buildings for his quarters: "They were dusty, musty, dirty, and looked as if they hadn't been occupied in years." Later the field was used as an Air Force Reserve Training Center. In 1954, it was renamed Bakalar Air Force Base to honor Lt. John Bakalar of nearby Hammond, Indiana, who was killed in aerial combat over France in September of 1944 while flying a P-51. The re-dedication ceremony was attended by the flyer's mother and his 11-year-old daughter, Suzanne, and 10-year-old son, Robert. Also attending was his widow, since remarried, Mrs. Dorothea Dugan.

The base was closed by the Department of Defense in January 1970. The city of Columbus received the title in 1972, and in 1982 renamed it Columbus Municipal Airport. Today, it is a first-class General Aviation airport, thanks to the excellent leadership of its manager, Mr. Wendell Ross. Some original buildings remain and are in use, although most are expected to be torn down by the late '90s. Additionally, an outstanding museum, the Atterbury Bakalar Air Museum, has been constructed and dedicated to the memory of all military and civilian personnel who served there during those difficult years.

Aerial view of Wakeman General Hospital, circa 1951. The hospital was closed after WW II and later reopened and upgraded during the Korean war. The building behind the circle on the bottom of the picture was the administration building. INDIANA NATIONAL GUARD

A view of the former administration building of Wakeman General Hospital, 1995. It is used as the headquarters for the Job Corps. Several buildings from the hospital remain, including the chapel, and the building housing the swimming pool. THOLE

Former chapel for Wakeman General Hospital patients. Today it sits alone and derelict.

BASIC TRAINING

···

Coffeyville Army Air Field

EARLY IN 1942, the War Department decided to build a basic training field outside the town of Coffeyville, Kansas, one of eleven Air Force bases the state would have before the end of World War Two. Coffeyville is in the extreme southeastern part of the state with the airbase being about three air miles northeast of the town. The airfield site was open land used for farming and oil drilling operations, and sat on about 1,440 acres. Coffeyville was an ideal site for a training field. Weather conditions were generally dry and clear with the worst weather occurring in December (52 percent unlimited ceilings) and the best, July (88 percent unlimited ceilings). There was very little fog. Three railroads and several major truck lines serviced the city.

The base was eagerly sought after by the town's community leaders. Many businessmen donated time and part of their expenses to get the base approved. Their efforts started in late 1941, with several visits by key city officials in Washington to talk with different agencies of the War Department. By Thanksgiving 1941, the Chamber of Commerce and the Airport Committee, received a commitment from the War Department for a site engineer to consider Coffeyville. Meanwhile the Chamber of Commerce prepared a survey of the many services, including electricity, water, and sewage, which would be needed if a base were located in Coffeyville. Coffeyville Army Air Field was one of the few bases heated by natural gas; most training fields used coal.

Visits to Washington were followed with letters pointing out the advantages of a field in Coffeyville. One example dated December 4, 1941, talked about water service being available "at the following rates in the event a squadron unit is located near our city." The Coffeyville Chamber of Commerce also sent a letter on December 5th describing available housing. It reads in part: "the Twenty one directors of the Coffeyville Chamber of Commerce have unanimously authorized a statement that 400 houses and apartments with the price range of $20 to $60 rent per month will be made available for officers of the proposed Tactical Bombing Squadron unit in Cof-

feyville." The state highway commission pledged it would build at their expense a two-lane concrete highway from the nearby U.S. Highway 169 to the base. Availability of workers to build the base was also considered. On March 20, 1942, a letter to the Chamber of Commerce from the United States Employment Service pointed out that a large nearby construction project was nearing completion. It said within "... three to five weeks there will be available about one thousand skilled workers, and three thousand semiskilled workers, and four thousand unskilled workers."

The decision was made to build the base, and on May 8, 1942, headlines of *The Coffeyville Daily Journal* screamed, "COFFEYVILLE GETS $7,000,000 U.S. ARMY AIR BASE." The Chamber of Commerce had intended to buy, with city funds, the 1500 acres necessary for the field, and then rent the land to the government for one dollar a year; however, this wasn't necessary, because the government bought the land immediately following condemnation proceedings. Construction began on June 10, 1942. It had really started before when the county began to improve the road network around the new base to handle the increased truck traffic hauling construction material to the site. The weather didn't cooperate, as the latter part of 1942 was very wet, slowing construction; however, most of the construction was accomplished over the next eight months. The construction project officer was Col. Carlisle J. Ferris who would also be the field's first commanding officer. His son Keith, lived there for a while as a young boy, and today is the well-known aviation artist. When finished, Coffeyville Army Air field had four runways, each 150 feet wide. The shortest was 5,872 feet. Most of the buildings were Theater of Operations construction while some were of the Mobilization type. The Mobilization type buildings included the station hospital, theater, chapel, and Link training buildings. There were three hangars with a parking apron a mile long and 450 feet wide. For administrative purposes the hangars were called, "North Stage, South Stage, and Central Stage." In effect, a new town had been con-

Aerial view of Coffeyville Army Air Field. The photo was taken in April 1945 at the height of the flood when the field was cut off from the city of Coffeyville. Training continued with the help of the many civilian workers who lived on the base during the flood. USAF

BT-13s from Coffeyville
in flight. TAYLOR

structed. Where before there had been only open farm land, this new city now contained 212 buildings, a water storage and distribution system, sewage system and treatment plant, electric transmission lines, a railway spur, and all the other things one could expect to find in a town of 5000 people. Its effect upon the city of Coffeyville (1941 metro population — 22,000) was dramatic.

The base was activated during June 1942 and named the "Army Air Forces Basic Flying School-Coffeyville Kansas." Later the name would be changed to "Coffeyville Army Air Field." It was the first of its type to be established in Kansas and would graduate the state's first class of cadets.

It was normal for a new base, built under extreme time pressure, to have start up problems. Coffeyville was no exception. Erwin Kaiser was an early arrival, who came during July 1942 from Enid Army Air Field, Enid, Oklahoma. However, there was no running water, and no roads. Coffeyville AAF wasn't ready for additional personnel. So he was sent back to Enid. Another early arrival, Eugene Woehl, was part of the 908th Quartermaster company. Eugene remembers that the base housing facilities were not ready. Some men were living under a baseball stadium at Forest Park, a recreation area in the city of Coffeyville. Meals were also served there for a time before the base mess hall opened.

The first large number of base support personnel, about 600 men, came to the field by train, arriving on September 18. The sewage system was not completed, and the water wasn't fit to drink because the pipes had not been cleaned. All drinking and cooking water had to be hauled from the city of Coffeyville in a street sprinkler. The electricity had been turned on and off intermittently during September, and came back on in the mess hall around 6 PM just as the troop train was backing into the siding. Due to a problem with the natural gas service, the first meal served at the base was barbecued wieners, instead of the originally planned roast beef. Dinner was about half finished when a cloudburst started. From then until January, the place was a sea of mud.

Lots of jobs needed to be finished before the cadets arrived. At the time, there was no water tower, so for fire protection, a fire truck was rented from the city of Coffeyville, and crewed by a driver and firefighter hired from the city. The post refrigeration units were not complete, meats and other perishables were stored in the Coffeyville Ice and Cold Storage company. Mr. Gordon allowed the base to use his shop, the City Meat Market, to prepare meat

The following three photos were taken from the field's water tower in October 1943, and give an excellent view of the field. The first building in the photo is the PX, the two large buildings behind it are the recreation building and the theater. The last large building in the distance is the chapel, which was located just inside the field's main entrance. USAF

View of the north end of the runway. The stockade is the building behind the fencing on the right edge of the photo. The buildings between the hangars are operations buildings and crew chief's buildings. USAF

Picture of the parachute loft with a hangar in the background. BT-13s are parked on the ramp. USAF

View of the headquarters building for Coffeyville Army Air Field, 1943. The flag pole foundation still exists today. This is a good example of Theater of Operations type construction. IRONSIDE

until facilities at the field were ready. Runways were not completed, nor were any of the maintenance buildings or shops in the sub-depot area. Most of the major construction would not be completed until January 1943.

Additionally, much remained to be built, i.e., taxiways, fencing, a crash station, a cadet operations building, some streets, and a civilian mess hall, etc. The fourth runway was started in July, later in August, the rebuilding of the original runways with concrete began.

So, as was typical with most of the training bases, training began while the field was being completed. The first group of cadets arrived on November 11, 1942, about six months from the start of construction. This was class 43-C with 137 members from primary flying schools at Muskogee, and Tulsa, Oklahoma. Training started on November 14. While in basic flying school the student pilot learned to fly a more advanced aircraft than he soloed in primary flight training. At the time, Basic was a 10-week course consisting of 70 hours flying, 94 hours in ground school, and 47 hours in military training. At the end of the basic training, the student

moved on to advanced flight training at another base.

The trainer used at Coffeyville, and at several other basic flying schools, was the Consolidated-Vultee BT-13 "Valiant." This was a single-engine (Pratt & Whitney 450 HP) low-wing, two-seat trainer with fixed gear. The Valiant, or "Vibrator" as many called it, had a maximum speed of 164 mph. and cruised at 140 mph. There were 11,537 produced before production stopped during the summer of 1944.

Coffeyville received its first BT-13s on November 8, just eight days before the start of flight training. Since construction of the maintenance hangars (there was difficulty getting metal for the hangars) was still in progress, maintenance was done outside on the parking ramp. Many mechanics wished they were some place else, because it wasn't pleasant working outside in the cold, rain, and snow of the early Kansas winter. To make matters more interesting, the sub-depot supply warehouses weren't finished, so parts were kept, and the sub-depot operated in the City of Coffeyville at the Ford dealership. At first, maintenance personnel had to make their own desks, tables, and work benches. Important maintenance equipment and aircraft parts were not available, so occasionally aircraft were cannibalized to keep the remainder flying. Maintenance went on day and night. Like flight training, maintenance procedures and organization were consistently reviewed and improved. Eventually, a base mechanics school was established. This along with the other improvements, led to about 96 percent of all aircraft being available for training by June 1943.

Early, only broad course objectives, requirements, and directives were received from higher headquarters. As time went by, these directives became more specific. As a result, the flight training program at Coffeyville continually changed. Additionally, training was hindered by lack of equipment, facilities, and trained personnel. Instrument training provides a good example of the continual evolution of training at Coffeyville. At first, all instructors gave their students the appropriate instrument training. Later, this phase of training was delegated to a few instructors who specialized in this phase of the cadets training. During the winter of 1943 and 1944, all instructors took additional training and became qualified to teach instrument flying. So, the centralized training for instruments was stopped. Many felt this was a positive move, because the student could stay with the same instructor throughout his training at Coffeyville. Later as directives became more specific, some instructors would complain about the lack of

· · ·

Sub-Depot maintenance hangar, 1943. The building still exists today and is used by a private firm. USAF

Sub-depot maintenance hangar as it is was in 1990. THOLE

South hangar in 1995, still in use and in excellent condition. INGMIRE

One of the three squadron hangars in 1943. This was the south hangar. USAF

Remains of flagpole foundation today, directly behind it was the post headquarters. INGMIRE

flexibility. Students were now required to spend a specific amount of time on specified maneuvers. One instructor felt "the emphasis is now placed on records and not on individual student training." Another would later comment, "One of the most glaring faults I find is the tendency to train the student for the sole purpose of meeting requirements." To help with instrument training, fifteen Link Trainers were put into operation in mid-December 1942 with Class 43-C. The course of instruction was 15 hours. One problem with the Link instructors was, they were trained at twelve different fields and so taught the course twelve different ways. Additionally, supplies were hard to get, and the training buildings were not suited for the task. A new building was built specifically for Link Training. By March 1944, there were thirty-four link trainers.

For a time, there were six training squadrons at the field, eventually this settled down to three, they were the 822nd, 823rd, and the 825th. Training ran Monday through Saturday. Sometimes it was necessary to schedule Sunday flying when inclement weather prevented flying during the week. Normal flying periods were one hour, except cross-country flights. Usually cross-country flights took place between Coffeyville and Claremore, Oklahoma, and Neosho, Joplin, and Nevada, Missouri. Others were flown between Coffeyville, Chanute, and Fort Scott, Kansas.

Flight training consisted of several subjects that included, takeoffs and landings, aerobatics, cross-country navigation, and night flying. Ground school involved navigation, meteorology, radio communications, and aircraft recognition. Normally ground school was given between flying lessons. Sometimes it was done in the very early AM or after the evening meal. Typically the day would start with Reveille at 6:15 AM, followed by breakfast at 6:30. Flying would begin at 7:45 AM. If a student was not scheduled to fly, he would be in ground school, drill, or involved in required athletics. By March 1943, the field had three control towers with three radio frequencies to help control student flights.

In late 1943, a special squadron was established for extra instruction of those cadets who might be saved from elimination with extra flying training. It was called "Squadron X," or more commonly known as "The Bumblebees." It achieved some success with a 70 percent graduation rate for the first sixty-one students held over.

Many ground school instructors had received commissions directly from civilian life, and after at-

Parachute loft as it was in 1995 after extensive restoration directed by Bob Ingmire (Airport/Industrial Park Coordinator) with labor and materials that were mostly donated. Further restoration is planned for the loft itself. INGMIRE

This is probably the remains of the Finance Office safe. The office was located in the same area as the post headquarters. INGMIRE

tending Officer Training School were sent to Coffeyville. 2nd Lt. Betz was one of these. Formerly an English professor at a women's college, he was sought by Air Force recruiters looking for instructors. He initially turned them down but after reconsidering, joined up. He would teach meteorology at Coffeyville. Lt. Betz held three college degrees, including a Ph.D. in English. Perhaps it was this degree that earned him the additional chore of assistant base historical officer. When Lt. Betz first started teaching, much needed equipment wasn't available. So adjustments were made, and some equipment like an opaque projector was borrowed from the Coffeyville High School. The projector was used for the aircraft recognition class, with pictures of planes cut from magazines.

Rufus Wysong was an instructor pilot at Coffeyville. He had just graduated from twin-engine school in November of 1943, and was hoping for either his first choice, a B-26, or his second, a B-25. His third choice was "no choice" and that's what he got. He was assigned to Randolph Field, Texas, for instructor training; however, when he arrived, the class was full, so he, along with four other pilots, was ordered directly to Coffeyville to begin instructing.

After he arrived, while walking back from the mess hall following dinner, Rufus saw something that impressed him with the hazards of his new job. Driving by was a flat-bed truck carrying the crashed remains of a BT-13. Rufus always had the feeling that to relax even for a moment while instructing could be fatal. It had been a long time since he had flown a BT-13, and then only as a struggling cadet. So, he and another newly assigned instructor, borrowed a BT-13 and managed about ten hours flight time to reacquaint themselves with the plane. Rufus was assigned to the 821st Training Squadron and started instructing on December the 5th.

Because he was a new instructor, Rufus had four students. The instructors who had been there longer sometimes would be assigned three. He would spend about four and a half hours in the air instructing, however some evenings his night training would start at 8 PM and end at 1 AM. Typically, the student would fly about two hours per day, one hour during the day and another at night. The remainder of the day would be spent in ground school and other activities. After six to seven hours instruction, the student would solo.

All Rufus's students eventually went on to graduate, however, some had unique problems. He remembers one who didn't seem to be able to count.

Sometimes toward the end of a flying session, he would ask the student to spin the plane to lose the excess altitude fast. This student had trouble remembering how many spins Rufus wanted. In one case, he told the cadet he wanted a two and a half turn power off spin and the cadet did three. This happened several times. So he took the plane to its maximum altitude, and then told the cadet he wanted fifteen spins. Fifteen spins later, the cadet made an excellent recovery. After that, he never seemed to have a counting problem. Rufus also remembers the bitter winter cold when temperatures often hovered near the zero mark. This combined with high winds sometimes made flying absolutely miserable. The BT-13 cockpit wasn't much help during those bitter cold days because the heater outlet was between the rudder pedals in the front cockpit. As a result, the instructor got very little heat in the rear of the plane. So there was little to be done except look forward to landing and the warmth of the operations building. The BT-13 was fully acrobatic, and all the normal acrobatic maneuvers were done along with some not in the books. One maneuver that was extremely popular was discovered quite by accident and after a while ended the same way. A pilot dove the plane as fast as possible and then after pulling out in a vertical climb at about 160 knots would do a vertical snap roll. It was great fun until one day a cadet snapped the tail off during the vertical roll. Both instructor and student parachuted to safety, the plane crashed with the engine bouncing across the field like a golf ball.

Later, in December, Rufus' wife joined him at Coffeyville where they rented a brand new home on the west side of the town. While there were not many restaurants, one was a particular favorite, because of its Filet Mignon special at ninety-nine cents. His last flight as an instructor was on April 13, 1944. From there, Rufus left for the South Pacific where he would spend a tour flying C-47s. Late in 1991, he attended a family reunion in Missouri and then drove on to visit Coffeyville. Standing on the parking apron in front of his old hangar, he visualized again the many BT-13s, some parked, others taxiing out to the runway. He also recalled with sadness the instructors and students who lost their lives while training at Coffeyville. The first cadet fatality at Coffeyville was Cadet Ray Mussack (Class 43-D) killed in a training flight. During the first thirteen training classes, Coffeyville AAF graduated 2,680 pilots, and there were 18 fatalities. In total, there were sixteen basic training classes, the last was Class 44-G

Interior view of the Post Exchange, 1943. USAF

Cadets studying in the "War Room," 1943. Most bases had a War Room that posted the latest news of the war world wide and other related information. USAF

finishing on May 24, 1944.

Life was not all work for the cadets. The first USO dance for enlisted men was held on March 4, 1943. The first formal social function for the cadets was a dance at Memorial Hall in Coffeyville. Also, a cadet club was opened in Coffeyville on West Eighth Street. A wives' club was formed and involved itself in many projects, the most important being welfare and Red Cross activities. This included helping the wives settle among strange surroundings, visiting cadets in the hospital, and decorating the cadet recreational buildings. The club met weekly and published a small mimeographed paper. The city of Coffeyville allowed the cadets to use the high school swimming pool, and reserved it for their use during part of the day. In addition, there were USO shows from time to time, and dances attended by invited guests from Coffeyville and surrounding communities. The first movies shown in the base theater were "Cooks and Crooks" and "The Navy Comes Through." Admission price was fifteen cents. The bowling alley was opened in May 1943 and had six lanes. The field had its own radio show that was arranged and written by the special service staff. Sometimes it broadcasted from Coffeyville on station KGGF. The field radio station went on national radio on June 25, 1943, with the Coca Cola "Victory Parade of Spotlight Bands." Golf was also available at reduced rates at Coffeyville's Hillcrest Country Club. The post had a gymnasium and several athletic fields for softball, football, and volleyball. No base was complete without its obstacle course and Coffeyville was no exception. The base newspaper, *Air Currents* proudly announced the obstacle course opening scheduled for December 7, 1942. The course was 440 yards long, oval in shape with eighteen obstacles. The athletic department planned to have every man on the post run it at least once per week. The base produced two Kansas State Golden Gloves boxing champions.

The last basic training class, 44-G, held their graduation dance in Coffeyville's Memorial Auditorium on May 20, 1944. At this point in the war, there was no longer the need for the vast numbers of new pilots being produced by the many training fields, so Coffeyville received notice to close down;

however, the base remained open when it was transferred from the Central Flying Command to the Third Air Force.

The field's new mission was to train photo reconnaissance pilots. The trainer would be the F-5, an unarmed photo recon version of the P-38. Also, some F-10s were used. This was the photo recon version of the B-25. During the field's first full year of training, June 1944 to June 1945, approximately 460 pilots were trained. This training continued through the end of the war, however the pace slowed. Finally on Tuesday morning, October 2, 1945, a telegram arrived from the War Department that said, "You are authorized to announce the temporary inactivation of Coffeyville Army Air Field, Coffeyville, Kansas on or about 1 October." All training stopped. The only exception was the completion of training for several Chinese students. The base newspaper, *Air Currents* published its last edition on October 12; it was the 48th issue, and was headlined, "Souvenir Inactivation Edition." The base closed gradually. Some buildings were sold and moved into town as temporary housing, one even found use as a bar. Excess supplies were hauled off to other bases, with the excess aviation gas going down the road to the nearby Independence Army Air Field, at Independence, Kansas.

The field was transferred to Tactical Air Command on March 21, 1946, and later to the U.S. District Engineers. Finally on July 21, 1947, during a two-day air show attended by over one thousand people, the field's name was changed from Coffeyville Municipal Airport to Harold McGugin Field. This was in honor of Mr. McGugin, who was a member of Congress and served in both World Wars I and II, reaching the grade of Lieutenant-Colonel. At the ceremony Mr. E.V. Tuney of the War Assets Administration made a formal presentation of the deed to the City of Coffeyville.

Today, Coffeyville's airfield remains in use and is the center of a growing industrial park. Unlike some former WW II training fields, it is in excellent condition. Several original buildings remain in use, including the sub-depot and the three original squadron hangars.

Building remains as they appeared in 1990. These derelict structures are being removed as part of the field's improvement program. The structure with the brush growing in it was probably the base finance office. THOLE

TRAINING B-17 PILOTS

Lockbourne Army Air Field

LOCKBOURNE Army Air Field, later renamed Rickenbacker Air Force Base, grew out of 1,600 acres of rich farm land located near the town of Lockbourne, Ohio. Lockbourne is about ten miles south of Columbus, Ohio, off State Route 317. Today, the air field is still surrounded by farm land, although the metro area of Columbus is creeping closer, and the location is not as isolated as it was fifty years ago.

As early as December 1941, local newspapers were announcing construction of the field. Some articles speculated the base might be part of a network of bases to aid in the rapid transfer of fighter planes from one coast to another in case of attack. Other newspaper reports said the field would be used as a training site for army bomber crews. This confusion was typical in the early days of training field construction. Much speculation went on in the towns near the soon to be constructed air field about the intended use of the field. Sometimes, a field's mission changed even as it was being constructed. In others, the purpose in building was clear from the outset and the base served the intended purpose. This was simply a function of the constantly changing requirements brought on by a frantic training program trying to meet the needs of a nation ill prepared for a world war.

As early as October 1941, an Army site selection board met at the field's purposed location. By January 1942, soil samples were being taken and engineers were at work. Toward late February, most of the farmers who formerly owned the land had moved. This was an extreme hardship for many farmers, especially those who had lived on the land for their whole lives. In all, about 50 owners and tenants had less than two months to move. Some land had been in the same family for generations, however they had little option but to accept the government's offer. Many of their homes were destroyed to make room for the airfield. Some buildings were converted for temporary use, while others sold to private individuals who moved them. Today, three of the homes, relocated in a later base expansion, are located next to each other near the entrance to the base.

Mel Eisaman spent part of his youth growing up on a farm that bordered the base next to the runways. He remembers much of the early building activity and the flying activities. Of the initial construction, he writes ". . . Of course no one wanted to give up their land and move; however, the government was paying an acceptable amount per acre and nearly everyone was resigned to the fact that the U.S. government could take what it wanted. I do recall one farmer, though, that just wasn't going to give in. His farm was located about one and a half miles north of our farm on the east side of the Ashville Pike. He was about 63 at the time and had put his whole life into that farm, and he just wasn't about to leave. He just sat tight and one day the bulldozer showed up to demolish his buildings. The dozer operator ran over and destroyed the fence on the way in, and was promptly met by the farmer wielding an ax handle. The farmer jumped up on the dozer and soon convinced the operator that his head might hurt for a long time if he chose to move the dozer another foot. The government finally convinced the farmer that he had to go, and he agreed to knuckle under if they would allow him time to move the house. So he bought a few acres and moved his house across and down the road. I think that he more or less retired then, and spent most of his time looking up the road at what used to be his farm and watching all the flying activity across the road to the east. It's rather sad though, as in 1951 when the government decided to expand the base, they again took his farm."

Construction began on April 4, but rain and mud prevented any serious building until May. Meanwhile, the Norfolk and Western railway had about 150 men putting down track from their main line at the nearby town of Lockbourne to the base. By September 30, the first phase of the field's construction was completed. With construction still going on, the field was activated on June 15, 1942. It would first serve as an advanced training base for glider pilots. The

Aerial view, Lockbourne Army Air Base, circa 1944. There are approximately 71 B-17s in the photo. SMITHSONIAN

Aerial view of the field taken in 1992. Buildings in lower right hand corner are the WW II Base Engineering Shop (Bldg. 530) and the Base Engineering Maintenance and Inspection building, (Bldg. 532). Bldg. 530 is the smaller of the two and was torn down in 1995, Bldg. 532 is being renovated. THOLE

Former post headquarters (Bldg. 1) as it was in 1995.
THOLE

. . .

This building is located next to today's control tower and was probably the Crash Truck Garage. It may have been Korean War era construction. THOLE

Base Engineering Maintenance and Inspection building (Bldg. 532) as it appeared circa 1945 USAF.

The same building as it was in 1995. THOLE

. . .

28

The Bomb Trainer Building (505) as it appeared in 1995. Here pilots were given training on proper bomb run approach procedures. THOLE

program was short lived, but proved important to the development of gliders as a major part of U.S. airpower. To better appreciate the part Lockbourne played, a brief review of the state of the U.S. Army Air Forces glider program in 1941 might be helpful.

Before 1941, the Army Air Corps had no formal glider training program and, of course, no glider pilots. In February 1941, the Air Corps, influenced by the German success with military gliders, began studies to develop such aircraft. The Japanese attack on Pearl Harbor put everything on a crash basis, including the development of a program to train glider pilots. The requirement for glider pilots dramatically increased over a short period. Just a few days after Pearl Harbor, it was placed at 1,000. This would increase to over 4,000 in April 1942, to 6,000 in May, and by October there were more than 10,000 men selected for glider pilot training.

It was decided to break the training into two phases, basic and advanced. The basic training would be done at civilian schools, and the student would then be sent to advanced training at a military base. The civilian schools were called Preliminary Light Airplane Gliding Schools, and as there were not enough gliders, instruction was given in light, single engine planes. Students were instructed in landings with the engine shut down. By June 1942, there were 18 schools involved in this type training. In an attempt to give some glider training in real gliders, the government issued purchase orders for two place gliders with several different manufacturers. Before this, an attempt was made to buy training gliders

from civilian owners, but in the entire U.S., only 61 were found, including some that were home built.

The shortage of gliders led to a decision to convert some small planes used by the Civilian Pilot Training Program. An Aeronca "Defender," a Taylorcraft "Tandem" and a Piper "Cub" were converted into the prototypes TG-5, TG-6, and TG-8 by removing the engine and adding another seat, making a three place training glider with tandem seating. In total, approximately 759 aircraft of this type were built. By October 1942, almost 6,000 students had been graduated from primary schools; however, for the most part, there was no place for them to go because of the lack of large combat gliders for advanced training.

Lockbourne was selected as one of the first fields to be used for advanced glider training. Training cadre began arriving in June 1942 while the field was being constructed, under the temporary command of Captain Robert F. Burnham. The field's first permanent commander, Lt. Colonel Ora M. Baldinger, assumed command in late June, and Captain Burnham became director of training. At one time, Captain Burnham was president of the Soaring Society of America and in 1944, he would return as a Colonel to again take command of the base.

The instructors were from Maxwell Field, Alabama, and had little in the way of glider training experience. They were chosen because they were flexible and could fit into this new program. In addition, there were several pilots who had just completed glider training at Elmira, N.Y. They would play

The following photos were taken in 1992 and show several former Lockbourne AAF buildings. They have since been removed as the facility is being converted to an industrial park. THOLE

Fire Station (Bldg. 300).

Post Office (Bldg. 3).

Igloo for black powder storage (Bldg. 614).

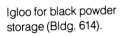

Base Engineering Shop
(Bldg. 530).

The former Post Engineer
Office (Bldg. 421) as it was
in 1995. THOLE

Foundation of a former
warehouse (Bldg. 536).
THOLE

. . .

31

Bldg. 593 was listed as the "target butt" on the field's basic layout plan and probably used to test fire or practice firing aircraft weapons during the war. Picture taken in 1994, the structure still exists, but is no longer used. THOLE

a key role in getting the program underway at Lockbourne.

Initially, there were two types of trainees at Lockbourne. The first group had graduated from basic glider training, and received advanced training at the field. The second group made up a glider "pool." At this point, the Air Force glider pilot recruiting program had produced too many approved cadets for the limited number of fields available to train them, so they were put into "pools" to await training. Lockbourne was also one of the holding bases, and by mid-September 1942, there were 1,139 men in the pool. This arrangement produced morale problems. There were no resources to adequately occupy their time, and they were frustrated with the delay in the start up of primary training.

Henry Jocz was a member of the glider pool at Lockbourne for about four months. He did not receive any glider training there, but remembered his time being occupied with sending and receiving code, meteorology courses, and commando training (state policeman gave judo instruction). Henry has fond memories of Columbus, Ohio, and the nearby town of Grove City. One Sunday stands out in his memory because many families from Grove City treated about 180 cadets to dinner in their homes, movies, bowling, and dancing. Later, Henry would be sent to Pittsburgh, Kansas, where he would begin his glider training.

Training for the advanced students ("Commandos of the Air") began Monday, July 6, 1942, and the first class, consisting of 20 enlisted men, and one officer, graduated Sunday, July 19. At this time, the field was still under construction and only a few buildings were completed. There were no paved roads or sidewalks, and mud was everywhere. Post headquarters was located in what later would be the finance office. Colonel Baldinger had two small rooms, one used for his office, the other for sleeping. He spent most of his time here. The hospital was not yet complete, and when a serious injury occurred on July 11, the student was taken by jeep to Fort Hayes, a military installation in Columbus, about 15 miles north of Lockbourne.

The duration and content of the program would change as more was learned about gliders and their use. At first, instructors and equipment were in extremely short supply, if they were available at all. Sometimes, gliders and instructors came direct from soaring clubs. Much of the course content, teaching procedures, and instructional aids were developed as training progressed. Early graduates received wings adapted from the standard pilots' wings by removing the shield and having a jeweler place a large "G" in its place.

The initial classes at Lockbourne were small, with less than a hundred students. The course lasted two weeks. Time was divided into ground classes, and soaring training. The first flights were in single seat gliders towed by a jeep down one of the 5,000-foot runways. When it had reached sufficient altitude, the glider was released to land on the remainder of the runway. After landing proficiency was mastered, the two-seat glider was used to teach soaring techniques. Frankfort TG-1 and the Schweizer TG-2 and TG-3 sailplanes were used for this training. At first, only small gliders were available and the entire course of flying instruction was given in that type. When the number of small gliders was insufficient for training, small single-engine planes were again used to practice dead-stick landings. Later, training in night flying was added to the program. This was challenging, because the field had no lights or radio equipment, and the tower was not operating. A hand-held signal light was used to help control traffic. The first two large military cargo/transport gliders (either CG-3As or the larger CG-4As) arrived at Lockbourne in August on a test flight from Wright Field, Dayton, Ohio. By mid-September, Lockbourne had a total of six CG-4As.

The CG-4A was, by the standard of the day, huge. The Waco Aircraft company was the design contractor for the CG-4A, and, along with 15 other companies, produced about 14,000. The aircraft could carry 13 fully equipped soldiers, a jeep with four man crew and equipment, or a 75mm howitzer and crew plus supplies and ammunition. It had a wingspan of over 83 feet and weighed almost 4,000 lbs. when empty. They were towed into the air by C-47s and were very forgiving in flight.

Besides learning to fly gliders, students were also required to attend class in several related subjects. This instruction included code, meteorology, navigation, aircraft identification, and instrument flying in the Link trainer. They were typically cram courses and did not go into any depth. Drill and calisthenics were also part of the two-week training. Although this was a new program with serious equipment shortages and few experienced personnel, it was successfully completed with no fatalities.

By September, it became clear that the rumors of moving the training to a different base were true. Lockbourne would end its involvement in glider training, and by October, the program was transferred to Stuttgart Army Air Field in Arkansas.

B-17 training started at Lockbourne with the arrival of several "Fortresses" from Hendricks Field, Sebring, Fla. They were loaded with 20 instructors and administrative officers, 39 student officers, and 102 enlisted personnel, plus some training aids. Six of the B-17s remained and training started on 15 January 1943 with some students flying that day.

There were then two different flying schools at Lockbourne. One was a nine-week course of four-engine pilot transition, and graduates were designated B-17 combat pilots. The other program was the Central Instructors School. Its objective was the training of instructors for assignment to B-17 pilot training schools throughout the AAF.

Since instructors were in such short supply, the first task at Lockbourne was to train the trainers. This started in January and ran until late March. Some students were trained as instructors for the B-17 schools at Hobbs Field, New Mexico, and Hendricks Field, Florida, the remainder stayed at Lockbourne. Ninety-one instructors were graduated during the January/March period. At this time the official designation of the field was "Pilot Transition School (Four-Engine)." The name would be changed in March and again in April to "Army Air Forces Pilot School (Specialized Four-Engine)."

Training began in earnest during March. By the end of the first ten months of the program, March 29, 1943, to late January 1944, 1,122 students had finished their instruction. Of this total, 555 graduated from the Central Instructors School and 1,367 became B-17 combat pilots. The average number of students in training during this period was about 370, with the peak being 506 students in August.

At first, because of the small number of instructors, all duty assignments were given orally by Col. A.R. Walker, director of training. Then, it was possible for all the officers to gather in one room to talk about problems and review their jobs. Additionally, during the start up of training, Col. Walker personally gave each student their check rides. Later, as more instructors became available, he began to delegate this responsibility.

With the buildup of instructors and material, the first pilot transition class started on March 29 with class 43-4B from Smyrna Army Air Base, Tennessee. Aircraft available for training had grown from the original six to over twenty, and in March alone, there were more than 3,000 hours flown. By February 1944, seventy-nine B-17s were assigned to the field.

The nine-week pilot transition course consisted of 105 hours of flying and ground school instruction. Included in the flying syllabus was instrument (40 hours), formation (5 hours) and navigation (25 hours). There were 15 hours of Link training. At first, there were few equipment mockups available as teaching aids. However, as time went by, more equipment became available, and instruction was more thorough. Many instructional aids were made by the base staff from crashed or derelict aircraft including engines, instruments, and aircraft systems.

The early training was not without cost in both men and material. During the first full year of training, from January 1943 to early February 1944 there were more than 40 deaths. As time went on, hard lessons were learned, and action taken to improve training safety for future students.

John Planck arrived at Lockbourne just before Christmas 1944, and for a brief period served as a flight engineer. He never received any formal training in this specialty; his training was given to him by a crew chief. John remembers spending most of his flying time sitting in the radio room of a B-17G and doing very little in the way of flight engineer duties. Each training crew had four or five officers aboard and they handled the flight engineer responsibility. The instructor acted as the command pilot. Many flights were four hours long, and some were longer. They were very noisy, often flown at night, and were uncomfortable. He recalls that often crews would reel out their 300 feet long trailing antenna and listen to commercial radio stations. More than one crew forgot to reel it in before landing. Sometimes crews would fly to the nearby Buckeye Lake and buzz it, attempting to swamp the sailboats.

The first class in the Central Instructors School was 43-H and started training on September 12, 1943. Central Instructors School was also a nine-week course. However, based upon the knowledge and skill showed, the student could graduate in as little as three weeks. The major difference between transition training and instructors' school was more flying, including day, night, instruments, and formation. There was additional training in blind takeoffs, and 15 hours less instruction in navigation.

At first there were no auxiliary fields used on a full time basis. Later, the Cleveland Municipal Airport, Dayton's field at Vandalia, Ohio, Clinton County Air Field, near Wilmington, Ohio, and a field near Richmond, Indiana, were used. In addition, a field was built southwest of Cincinnati, Ohio, as part of the auxiliary network. It had four 5,500 ft. runways but no control tower. Today, this field is the Greater Cincinnati-Northern Kentucky Airport.

Mel Eisaman remembers an accident while the B-17s were practicing landings ". . . one day, hiking to my favorite post, I emerged on the east side of Barch's Woods to see a B-17 laying on its belly in the field. It had wiped out my favorite post on the way to a sliding stop a few hundred yards south of the base. It seems that on the night before, this aircraft was shooting landings and the pilot was directed to go around as he was too close to the aircraft ahead. On the go-around, he saw the lights at the south end of the runway and thought them to be the other aircraft. It seemed best to go under the other aircraft as he was overtaking rapidly. Too late, he realized he was trying to go under the runway end lights and

he struck the ground, bounced, striking and wiping out the post and then bellied-in the field east of the woods. All on board, escaped serious injury." Mel recalls ". . . it was common to get a wave from a flight engineer standing in the waist window as they passed overhead, especially with two young gals waving back. On one pass the flight engineer not only waved but threw something out the window. It turned out to be a note weighted down with a flashlight battery. The note was a request for dates, names, phone numbers, etc. My sister's girlfriend later married the guy that threw out the note."

In March 1944, the nine-week transition course was extended to ten; Class, 44-4G was the first to take the extended training. Flying training on Sunday was stopped in July. Later, in August, the course was further expanded to 15 weeks. The added five-week "pre-transition" training was intended to help the student become more familiar with the B-17. Also, extra time was spent on navigation, maintenance, the duties of the aircraft commander, and gunnery familiarization training.

A continuing problem, was the maintenance of the aircraft. The field had four hangars that could house one aircraft each and one larger hangar that could handle three. Additionally, weather was a problem during the winter months, as was the continual shortage of trained personnel. As men returned from combat tours, personnel from the training bases experienced in such areas as maintenance, administration, ordnance, mess etc., were sent overseas to replace them. The difficulty in replacing their experience was obvious. For a while the shoe repair facility was closed because of the lack of trained personnel. Later most of the Link trainer operators were transferred, and some students were graduated with less than the required Link time.

At one point, training was going on day and night, 24 hours a day. Each plane was liable to fly three five-hour missions per day, and by September 1944, there were 84 B-17s used for training at Lockbourne. During October, the base handled 16,000 landings. As to be expected, there were many near accidents and times when death was averted by what could only be described as a miracle. Dave Bellmore recalls one of his night landings, when he came in behind two other B-17s simultaneously in the dark, on the same runway. The turbulence from the planes in front almost caused him to lose control, but somehow he managed to avoid the other aircraft. After landing, he expected to find grass stains on his wingtips.

Early glider training, gliders would be towed into the air by a jeep from one end of the runway, and then landed on the other end. USAF

WASPs on the flight line, they are E. Helen Dettweiler, Lucille F. Friesen, Mary E. Gair, the fourth is unidentified. USAF

Class in session, cadets are attempting to learn the mysteries of Morse code. USAF

Students working with the bomb trainer device. USAF

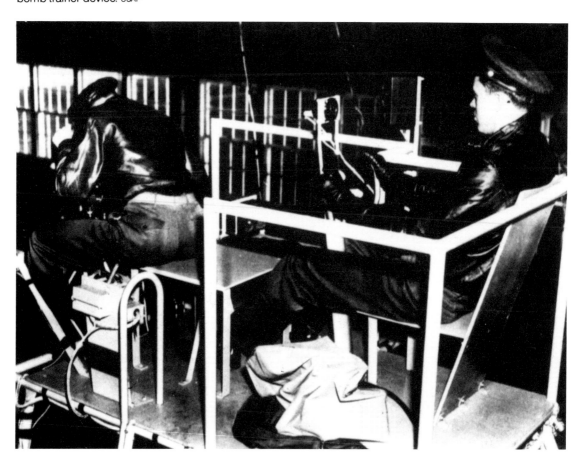

. . .

Hangar exterior view, this was a double hangar that could handle 3 B-17s. There were four additional hangars, each of which could take one B-17. USAF

The field became part of the WASP (Women Airforce Service Pilots) program in late 1944, when it was decided to set up an experimental program to train women to be four-engine bomber pilots. If they were successful, the graduates would fly B-17s in noncombat roles, thus releasing male pilots for combat. While there were other WASPs who flew B-17s, this was the only formal training designed for that purpose.

The trainees had recently completed the basic and advanced program at Avenger Field in Sweetwater, Texas, and were personally selected by Jacqueline Cochran, from a list prepared by the commanding officer of Avenger Field. The key factors were maturity, scores achieved during the Cessna AT-17 qualification, and conformance to height and weight limits. Their average age was about 26, none weighed more than 140 lbs., and few possessed more than 200 hours flight time.

The WASPs lived in the nurses' quarters, ate meals at the Officers' Mess, and took the standard transition course; however, the training period was extended from nine to twelve weeks. The extra time was needed because it was felt their prior training had not been sufficient to prepare them to fly the B-17. Training began on October 17, and was completed on January 15, 1944. The average flying time in the B-17 was 130 hours. No WASP was involved in an aircraft accident while at Lockbourne.

Dawn Rochow has good memories of her training at Lockbourne. She recalls her first training flight, when an engine caught fire, and how well the ship handled on the remaining three engines. Later, she would be required to fly, and often land, with only two engines running. While she found it difficult to exert the necessary pressure on the control surfaces to overcome the loss of power, she soon developed the necessary skills. As a Christmas present, Dawn's instructor, Col. Fred Wilson, gave each of his WASP students a silver dollar with miniature pilot wings attached. She still has those wings today.

There were 17 women assigned to the program, and they arrived at Lockbourne in October. Thirteen completed the training and became B-17 pilots. Nine were transferred to Buckingham AAF, Fort Myers, Florida, where they flew as co-pilots on B-17s for gunnery training missions. The other four remained at Lockbourne and took the Central Instructors School course. After they completed this additional training, they worked in the engineering department. Here they flew test flights, slow timed engines, and flew ferry trips.

· · ·

In general, the WASP program at Lockbourne was very successful. Their attitude was summarized by the comments of Peg Kirchner in a local newspaper: ". . . We couldn't believe it until we arrived at Lockbourne and saw those B-17s we had been chosen to fly. At first they looked so big to us, but now handling them is an everyday affair."

Training at Lockbourne continued through the end of the war until September 11, 1945, when flight training stopped. During this time, a total of 6,764 pilots were trained, 2,956 as instructor pilots. From the start of B-17 training through June 1945, the B-17s of Lockbourne flew a total of 322,258 hours, which at 170 mph is over 61 million miles. During this same period, there were a total of 68 B-17 accidents with 56 fatalities. On September 29, the base passed from the control of the Eastern Flying Training Command to the Air Technical Service Command. With the end of flight training, most of the B-17s (about 57) were flown to Hendricks Field, and approximately 35 were ferried to Walnut Ridge, Arizona, for storage. During this period, Lockbourne had six base commanders, Cols. O.M. Baldinger, A.C. Foulk, J.S. Gullet, A.R. Walker, and R.F. Burnham, and Lt. Col. B. F. McConnell.

Over the years, between the end of World War II and today, Lockbourne Army Air Base would undergo several major expansions, be deactivated and reactivated, shift from Air Force control to National Guard, and have its name changed to Rickenbacker Air Force Base. In operation for over 50 years, the base has been the home for fledgling glider pilots, four-engined bomber pilots, units of the Strategic Air Command, Tactical Air Command, Air Defense Command, the Air Force Reserve, Ohio National Guard, Naval Reserve, and the Seabees. For a while, it was home for the 477th composite Group (Tuskegee Airman) commanded by Col. Benjamin O. Davis. The base has participated in World War II, the Korean War, Vietnam, and Operation Desert Storm.

Today, most of the land occupied by Lockbourne Army Air Field has been taken over by the Rickenbacker Port Authority. It's slowly being developed into a first-class industrial park. Most of the WW II buildings are gone, replaced by sizable distribution centers and other buildings. A large air freight company uses the runways, and some of the former SAC hangars for its operations. Some buildings that remain are the base headquarters, a maintenance hangar and a large hangar. Across the field, a huge machine gun test bunker and a few other buildings sit. Most will be razed as the Port Authority continues its building program.

Many structures built during the Korean War, and the Vietnam War remain. The former base hospital sits derelict along with the SAC alert facility, and other buildings constructed during the later expansion and upgrade programs. The Air National Guard continues to serve here, occupying a small part of the former base. However, its presence continues to shrink, as it suffers from the current decline in funding for national defense.

Lineup of early training gliders on the flight line. USAF

· · ·

The Telephone Center (Bldg. 333) viewed in 1995. THOLE

Starting from the right, the Carpenter, Electric and Refrigeration Shop (Bldg. 422) rear view of the Post Engineer Office (Bldg. 421) and the Post Engineer Warehouse (Bldg. 423). Photo taken in 1995. THOLE

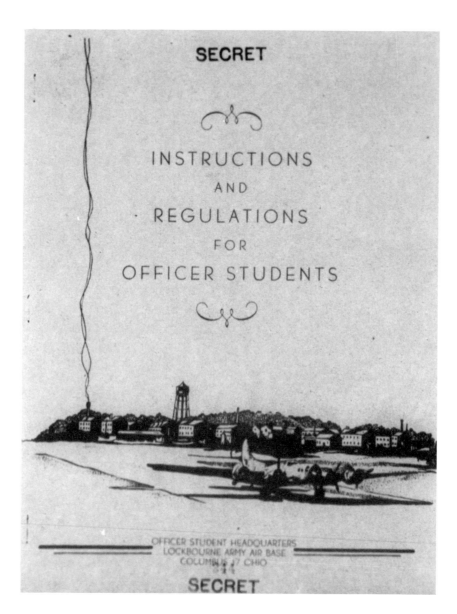

Book cover for student guide. USAF

GROUP TRAINING

· ·

Fairmont Army Air Field

DRIVE NORTH on State Route 81 out of Geneva, Nebraska, and after a few miles on the right you will see what remains of an important part of Air Force history. In the distance, over rows of corn, are visible the tops of three large hangars. Hangars big enough to enclose the B-24s, and B-29s that once roared down the runways, and parked on the hardstand here at Fairmont Army Air Field. Today's entrance is marked by a sign that tells you Fairmont Army Air Field is now Fairmont State Airfield.

Turn right onto the gravel road, and after about a mile you'll cross a runway, one of the three that remain. Soon you're on the windswept, deserted hardstand that stretches in the distance in front of the three squadron hangars. It's quiet now, not like it must have been when members of the 451st Bombardment Group (heavy) arrived here in September 1943 for Final Phase Training with B-24s. Off behind the hangars is the former base water tower, the tallest structure then as now. It stands silently, overlooking the area where the base hospital, barracks, motor pool, PX, movie theater, and many other buildings once stood. The buildings are gone now, as are the young men who once made this 1,980-acre base their temporary home on the way to the skies over Europe and Japan.

Corn grows where once stood the barracks housing the almost 6,000 officers and enlisted men, some assigned permanently, others making up the groups being trained. Directly behind the water tower was the base hospital, then a large 350-bed facility. It served Fairmont, and the nearby air bases at Bruning and Harvard, Nebraska. In 1943, this was the largest hospital in Nebraska. The base commander's home is still here, sitting by itself on the edge of the field overlooking what was the base warehouse area. The house is empty now, a victim of time and neglect. Then, as now, a gravel road ran past the house. Today there is little traffic. Occasionally a car will go by and from time to time a small plane, usually a crop duster, will use what is left of the runways, landing to refuel or refill its tanks with chemicals.

World War II was nine months old when a small article appeared in the September 3, 1942, edition of the *Nebraska Signal*. It read, "Prospects of Filmore County having an Army airplane refueling base became more definite Saturday when several Army officers came to Geneva to establish offices." Actually, by this time, the surveyors had been working for several weeks. Some of this work was done near the farms of Fred Baker and Bob Holsey and it included taking soil samples and checking the availability of a good supply of water.

Things moved quickly after the article appeared. By September 17, construction contracts had been signed and offices opened in the nearby town of Fairmont for the architect-engineering company of Wyatt Hedrich and Major Bert Burgivin of the Army Corps of Engineers. The affected farmers had until September 26 to retain possession of their homes and other buildings.

Housing availability would always be a problem for the construction workers, as it was later for military personnel and their dependents. As early as the beginning of September, workers were seeking living quarters in the nearby towns of Geneva and Fairmont whose population in 1940 was 1,888 and 800 each. Plans were made for establishing a trailer camp at the Geneva Fair Ground, and the Geneva Woman's Club began a survey of housing units for rent. The Bushman Construction Co. took over a former Safeway Grocery store and set up sleeping quarters for fifty men. Another store was converted to a commissary to help feed the construction workers when regular restaurants were closed. Construction would go on around the clock, with one shift ending at 2 AM and another beginning at 6 AM. On the edge of Geneva a "temporary" housing project of frame barracks-type buildings was put up to help accommodate construction workers and their families. Later it was used for housing of married personnel stationed at Fairmont.

As late as August 1944, homes that before the war were renting for forty dollars a month were rented for $100.00 a month and sometimes more. Bedrooms,

Gunnery School building, circa 1944. USAF

As late as 1995, four hangars still existed at Fairmont Army Air Field. This picture was taken in 1989. THOLE

sometimes, were rented for as much as $12.00 a week. Making matters worse, two additional airfields, Harvard and Bruning, were being built simultaneously, each within 30 miles of Fairmont.

Construction of Fairmont was scheduled to begin on September 16, 1942, but not much was done that day because of rain, so it began in earnest the next. A railroad spur was built next to the construction site and for a time fifty carloads of construction material were used per day. Approximately 1,000 workers were employed. During the early phase of construction the base was called Fairmont Satellite Airfield. The parent base was the Topeka Army Air base at Topeka, Kansas. Early in 1943, the name was changed to Fairmont Army Air Field. At this time, a major expansion was announced to support the field's new mission as a final phase training facility

for heavy bomber groups. Runways were lengthened, additional buildings constructed, and later four celestial navigation training buildings built.

The first military personnel arrived around noon on November 10, 1942, under the direction of Quartermaster corps officer, 2nd Lt. William Prince, Jr. The small group of six men was an advance party and they would pave the way for the thousands to follow. They visited several businesses in the surrounding towns to sign contracts for bread, milk, and other needs. They also coordinated the handling of supplies arriving from the Kansas City Quartermaster Depot. At this time, there were no transient sleeping facilities at Fairmont, so their first night was spent at the Mc Cloud Hotel in York, twenty-one miles north of Fairmont. Later, Dan's Hotel in Geneva would be used because it had washing facilities in the basement. Meals were eaten in the various cafes around Geneva. Often the men were invited into homes in Geneva for meals and use of bathing facilities.

The first civilian, Ted Everts, was employed on November 23 and he along with several others worked at trucking supplies to and from the field. Mrs. Dorothy Bunker lives in the nearby town of Milligan and was one of the earliest civilian employees. She would be at the base for its opening, and the closing. Dorothy met her husband, Jim, at the nearby Bruning Army Air Field and they were the last couple married at the base chapel at Bruning. Dorothy worked for Lieutenant Prince and spent much of her time typing purchase orders, requisitions for building materials, and payrolls for the construction workers. For a while she also handled the switchboard. One of the earliest purchase orders was dated December 28, 1942, for 21,350 quarts of milk at 14 cents per quart from the Fairmont Creamery Co. Requisition Sheet No. 1 was dated October 25, 1942, and showed the field was authorized 1,202 officers and enlisted men. Items such as "spoon, table, 1,262," "pitchers, water, 5 qt.," and "cots folding steel, 1,250" were ordered.

At this point, the field was still under construction and Dorothy remembers everything being "knee deep in mud." Construction workers came from many different places, some from bases just completed. Local people also helped with the building during the day, then at night would work their farms. The field was completed in November with just a few carpenters left doing finishing jobs. Many workers returned in late spring to complete the base expansion. By December, there were approximately 75 military personnel on base, with the first large numbers arriving in January 1943 when the field was ready for operations.

A base newspaper, *The Dust Bowl Sand Sock*, first appeared in April 1943. The name was later changed to *Fairmont Army Air Field News*. Items about the base were printed, as was war news from all over the world. The paper was intended to keep the personnel informed and to be sent to let family and friends know about the happenings at Fairmont.

The May 20, 1944, issue advertised the current movies at the base theater, *Silent Partner And the Angels Sing*, starring Dorothy Lamour and Fred McMurray. Thursday's and Friday's feature was *Once Upon a Time* with Cary Grant. Matinees were at 2:30 PM, evening showings at 6:00 and 8:00 PM. There was a double feature on Saturday. The same issue talked about the importance of "giving prompt consideration to the advisability of making a will."

Service Club activities were a regular feature. The schedule for the week of May 13 was bingo on Saturday, variety show on Sunday, a dance on Tuesday, movies on Wednesday, a square dance on Thursday, and a dance on Friday attended by young ladies from the USO.

The first significant training started in August 1943 when a B-24 Standardization School was established at Fairmont. However, this was short lived, because in September it was moved to make room the 451st Bombardment Group (H). It would be followed by the 485th, 504th, 16th, and for a short time the 98th, 467th, and the 489th.

The 451st and 485th would train with B-24s, the 504th and 16th with B-29s, and the 98th, 467th and 489th were groups returning from Europe for training on B-29s. The 451st came from Windover Field, Utah, and left in November. The group operated with the Fifteenth Air Force and bombed aircraft factories, bridges, and airfields throughout Europe. The group received three Distinguished Unit Citations for its performance on raids to Regensburg, Ploesti, and Vienna.

With the arrival of the 451st, the base activity significantly increased as did the number of personnel. Total military assigned to Fairmont in November was 3,732. Training of these groups was final phase training before the group was sent to a staging area, then to a combat zone. Each group's training varied slightly, both in time and content, depending upon the war situation at the time. Each group was self-contained, with its own doctors, cooks, mechanics, etc., assigned and doing their responsibilities within the group. Each person came to Fairmont already trained in his specialty and now they would be joined to practice as a group and refine their skills. Additional training in gunnery, navigation, formation flying, bombing, etc., was given by the personnel permanently assigned to Fairmont. People in the communities became accustomed to the new base and frequently invited the soldiers into their homes for dinner. Young women under the supervision of the local USO often attended the Friday night dances. Many servicemen who met their wives here returned after the war to raise their families. Farmers were at first concerned that the noise from the bomber's engines would bother their cattle and chickens. However, the animals soon became accustomed to the noise and went about as usual.

Accidents happened both in the air and on the

Frontal view of two of the still existing four hangars as they looked in 1989. ERET

ground. The 451st had the worst air accident when at about 4:30 PM on October 25, 1943, two B-24s collided at 20,000 feet. Seventeen men were killed and one survived. This was a particularly sad happening because the flight was to be one of the last before finishing training. Most of the men's wives and girlfriends were waiting at the PX when the accident happened. In all, the 451st lost 22 crewmembers while training at Fairmont.

The 485th Bomb Group followed the 451st and began arriving in late October, 1943. Housing continued to be a problem, with some homes valued at $500.00 renting for $50.00 per month. The 485th completed training in March 1944 and moved to the

Rear view of hangars, empty field was former barracks area. THOLE

Mediterranean Theater flying B-24s. The group took additional training in Tunisia before going to Italy. One-half of the 831st Squadron, eight officers and 146 men were lost while moving from Africa to Italy. A torpedo attack on their troop ship took a total of 498 lives. Later, the 485th would win a Distinguished Unit Citation for its attack on an oil refinery at Vienna.

The first group to take B-29 training at Fairmont was the 504th, and it began arriving in March 1944. There were few B-29s available anywhere for training, so most of the group's early work was done in reconditioned, war-weary B-17s. At this time, B-29s were considered an elite operation. Pilots had to have considerable flying time before being assigned command of a B-29.

Tom Harker had about 450 hours as a B-17 command pilot before being sent to Fairmont for his B-29 training. Formerly, he was an instructor of the AAF School of Applied Tactics at Orlando, Florida. Tom left Fairmont with the 504th and flew 35 missions out of Tinian. Of his training at Fairmont, Tom remembers having only about five to ten landings and takeoffs in the B-29 before he soloed. For his solo, he took off in the afternoon and did not return until after dark. Tom never did get his long-range 3,000-mile practice mission. This was accomplished on the way to Tinian. The crews and planes were urgently needed in the Pacific. There simply was not sufficient time or planes to be as thorough as everyone would have liked. Tom's crew flew navigation missions to Puerto Rico and to Cuba's Batista Field, and then out over the gulf of Mexico for additional navigation practice.

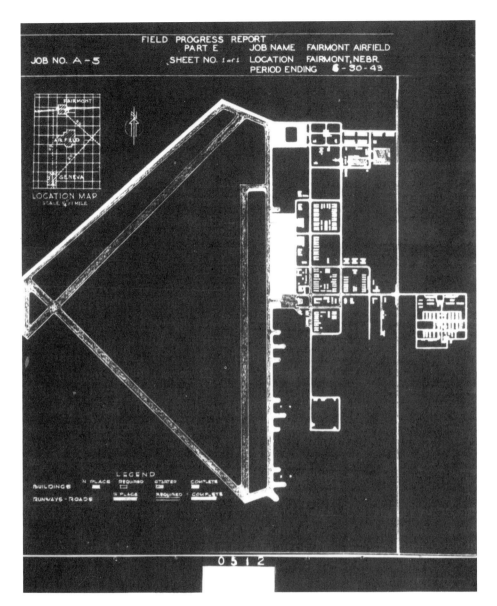

Photo for a progress report showing Fairmont's proposed and completed structures as of June 1943. USAF

Mural from EM's Service Club, painted by Pfc. Edward Flinsky. After the war, the building was sold and moved to a new location. There it was used as a church hall. While the building was being torn down in 1987, the mural was found on the back of a wall section. KLEINSCHMIT

. . .

Fairmont open house,
August 1944. Approxi-
mately 900 people
attended. This view shows
the photographic section's
exhibit. USAF

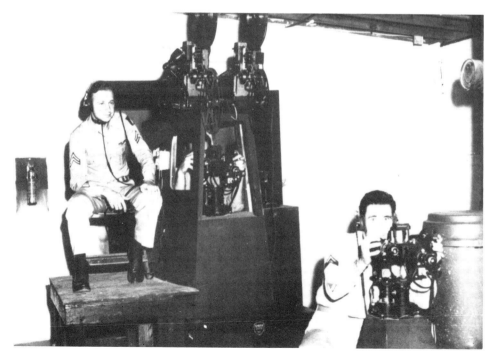

Gunnery school classroom.
This was probably a fire
control class on the B-29
gunnery system. Note
cameras in use. USAF

Photo taken in 1994, showing remains of foundation for the navigation training tower. One of four at Fairmont. ERET

One of the remaining runways as it appeared in 1989. The airfield is still in use as a state airfield and for agriculture spraying operations. THOLE

Former housing units in Geneva, Nebraska, as they were in 1989. The housing was built for construction workers and later used by married personnel stationed at Fairmont Army Air Field. Later on, following the war, the buildings were used for low income housing and were finally razed in the '90s. The single larger building was part of the same complex and was still standing in 1995. It was probably an administration or commons type building, perhaps used for the washing of clothing or bathing. THOLE

The former base chapel at Fairmont Army Air Field. After the war it was moved to Friend, Nebraska, where it was used as the Friend Berean Church. Army chapels were of a standardized design, this chapel is typical. ERET

A 1989 view of the former base commander's home. It still existed in 1995; however, it has been vandalized. THOLE

Hampering training was the lack of B-29s, parts, and personnel (especially navigators), plus the inability of the war-weary B-17s to gain high altitude. Training mockups were lacking, as well as radar sets. Also, the B-29 required 4.3 hours maintenance for each hour's flight, versus the B-17's 2.4 hours.

Besides training in the air, the group received ground instruction in many subjects including gunnery. Gunnery training was given on the B-29's Central Fire Control System both for maintenance men and gunners. In one month, 20,000 feet of film was used to give gunners practice tracking. Instruction on the B-29 Fire Control System was given by technical representatives from the General Electric Company.

In September 1944 (then) Lt. Col. Paul Tibbets visited Fairmont and selected the 393rd Bomb Squadron of the 504th Bomb Group to become part of his 509th Composite Group. The squadron left for further training at Wendover Field, Utah. Part of the squadron flew to Utah, while the ground personnel left Fairmont on a troop train at night. They left without their friends knowing where they had gone.

The Geneva USO started its operation in May 1943 and was located in the Geneva City Auditorium. It was open on Sunday afternoons and in the evenings from 6 PM until the last bus left for the base at 12:10 AM. The USO was a place to get away from the base. Men visited it to write letters, play games such as ping pong, listen to music, meet friends, or just talk with the volunteer hostesses. The hostesses often helped with marriage arrangements and find-

ing rooms in town for visiting wives, friends, and relatives. The USO was also used by wives and girlfriends, and the weekly attendance was usually over 3,000. Weekly dances were held Monday nights, sponsored by a local church and the American Legion. The women of the USO also helped in chaperoning the young ladies who went to the field for the Friday night dances at the Service Club. They also visited the field hospital, and while at the Service Club did mending and sewing on of insignia. They often took homemade cookies, candy and flowers to the base.

People from the surrounding area went out of their way to make the servicemen's stay at Fairmont more pleasant, and to make them feel welcome. Men from the larger cities were especially impressed with the warm, open hospitality of the townspeople. After leaving Fairmont, many service personnel wrote letters expressing their appreciation for the kindness shown. Here is an excerpt from a letter written by the wife of a soldier stationed for a while at Fairmont, ". . . I know I would have been very lonely if I had not felt that I was welcome to make use of the USO facilities. I spent part of every day there and many evenings, sewing, reading, playing the piano, or playing cards. I made many friends among the soldiers' wives through contacts at the USO. During my three years as an 'army wife,' I have traveled a lot but I have never been anywhere where people were as kind and friendly and as interested in the welfare of the serviceman and his wife as they are in Geneva. People were especially kind to me after my baby was born. I wanted you to know just how much the USO

Hangar under construction. Note the extensive use of wood. USAF

meant to me, and that it made a lonely soldier's wife much happier." Another wife of a solider wrote, "While there I lived at the home of Mrs. Verle Wilson who was the sweetest landlady I've ever had. She made all of her roomers feel at home and was like a mother to all of us far away from home."

The last B-29 group at Fairmont was the 16th and it began arriving on August 15, 1944, while the 504th was in the process of leaving. The 16th then left in March of 1945, and moved to Guam to fly missions over Japan. This group also won a Distinguished Unit Citation.

After the departure of the 16th Bomb Group, things slowed a bit because there was no tactical unit to train. The length of the work day shortened and passes were easier to get. During this time, personnel at the base received refresher training. Some were sent to other bases to help with the training there. A long list was prepared for a general cleaning up and repair of buildings on the base.

One project during this period was to decide how to replace the large amount of missing tools assigned to the maintenance personnel. There were two options, have the men pay for replacement via a "Report of Survey" or "find" the tools. It was decided to "find"

the tools. So barracks were searched and tools picked up at the various hangars and shops. When this was completed, there were more tools collected then had been listed as loaned out. Another project was to repair the bombing range at Silver Creek, Nebraska. Fencing was repaired and improved, stray cattle removed, and the 300- and 500-foot bomb circles were graded and limed. The target shack was also repaired.

During the May through July 1945 period, three groups returning from combat tours were assigned to Fairmont for training with the B-29. They were the 98th from the 15th Air Force and the 467th and 489th from the 8th Air Force, all of which had used the B-24. Their stay was short because at this point it was becoming clear that they would not be needed. The number of people stationed at the field in August was 2,762 military and 650 civilians.

On September 27, the War Department announced that on October 31 the field would go on temporary inactive status. So preparations were made to shut down Fairmont. It was done in several phases. The first part was to survey each department to decide how much time and resources it would take to inactivate the department. Then, the material was dismantled, packed, shipped out, or placed in storage. Final reports were prepared, personnel reductions continued, and a last inspection made. Much of the material was temporarily stored at Fairmont, but there was not sufficient warehouse space, so two hangars were used.

There was some hope that Fairmont might be kept open and made a permanent installation. So a representative of the towns around Fairmont went to Washington to help sell the idea of keeping the base open. The discussions were held with Gen. H. H. Arnold's Chief of Staff. However, the decision to close Fairmont was not changed and the process to remove equipment and buildings began in earnest. In November, Major Bixby of Geneva attended a meeting in Lincoln, Nebraska, called by the Governor to discuss the future of Fairmont and six other fields in the state scheduled to be closed. Then, the government was offering the airfields with their equipment to the municipal authorities for one dollar. Geneva did not accept the offer because of the expense that might be required to maintain buildings and equipment.

The field was declared surplus in the spring of 1946. Some equipment was given to the various schools; for example, the Geneva High School received considerable shop equipment including a drill press, lathes, band saws, grinders, etc. Much material was sold in lots. A sale of surplus property was open to the public, and was held on October 7 through 11 at the field. There were about 275 small lots that included items such as office furniture, office supplies, small hand tools, beds, mattresses, photo equipment, and farm machinery. Some unsold material such as typewriters and eating utensils was dumped in a trench and buried. Buildings were dismantled and the lumber sold by the truckload for one dollar. Other buildings were taken down and rebuilt at different locations. In 1947, one building, the Enlisted Men's Service Club, was dismantled and rebuilt at St. Mary's Church in Shickley, Nebraska, a town about 20 miles from Fairmont. The building was used as a church hall for about 40 years and then torn down. While it was being dismantled a painting was discovered on the backside of a wall board. It was a mural depicting several airmen against a backdrop of an American flag and some tall buildings. Two airmen who appear to be gunners and several others are doing various maintenance tasks. The painting was saved and is being kept by the people who purchased the former church hall.

Today, Fairmont is owned by the state. Much of it has been sold and a large part leased for agriculture purposes. One runway remains in use and is visited from time to time by an occasional aircraft.

This historic marker is located near today's entrance to the field along State Highway #81. It was put up by the Nebraska State Historical Society, the Fillmore County Historical Society, and the 451st Bombardment Group. ERET

. . .

B-29s FOR JAPAN

....

Herington Army Air Field

THE BOEING B-29 was born in Seattle, Washington, but for the most part, was raised in Kansas and went to war from there. The B-29 was a significant factor in making the invasion of Japan unnecessary.

Sprinkled across the state of Kansas were at least 12 major Army Air Fields; counting satellite and auxiliary fields, the total exceeded 30. Involved with the B-29 was Boeing's field at Wichita, and the Army Air Fields at Pratt, Walker, Great Bend, Smoky Hill, Salina, Topeka, and Herington.

Before the first B-29 would see Herington, major production and design problems had to be solved. This was typical of many combat aircraft produced during this period. However, the problems encountered with the Superfortress were unique because of the many innovations incorporated into its design, and the desperate need to get it into production. It was only one of two U.S. bombers ordered into production before the prototype was finished. The B-29 was the first bomber to have a pressurized crew compartment, remotely controlled gun turrets, and the new Wright R-3350 engine producing 2,200 horse power. It could deliver 20,000 lbs. of bombs and had a service ceiling of over 31,000 feet. Factories had to be built to produce it, and thousands of unskilled workers trained to work on the production lines. As expected, there were many changes and modifications necessary before the aircraft would be ready for combat. This was done at modification centers located in several areas of the country. Most of the changes centered on engine improvements, the defensive fire control system, and aircraft pressurization.

While all this was going on, the decision was made in Washington in November 1943 to use the aircraft against Japan. Later, the 20th Bomber Command was formed to take the 175 B-29s of the 58th Bomb wing to China through India for the first sustained bombing attacks upon Japan. General H. "Hap" Arnold was in charge of the project, and he wanted his B-29s to be ready by the end of February 1944. When he visited the 58th Bomb Wing headquarters at Smoky Hill Army Air Field in Salina, Kansas, in late January,

he was told that the aircraft would not be ready for several months. The problems were the same that had plagued B-29 production from the beginning. Modifications had to be made, parts were missing, systems did not work, and there were not enough skilled people to get the job finished on time.

This situation started the "Battle of Kansas." Modification centers were set up at Smoky Hill, Pratt, Walker and Great Bend Army Air Fields. They were all in Kansas, and relatively close to each other. The project was given top priority, and people and parts were brought in from all over the country. Most of the work was done outside, in the middle of a bitter cold Kansas winter. The "Battle" began in early March and was finished by mid-April. In all, about fifty modifications had to be done on each aircraft. It was an extremely difficult operation, performed by people working sixteen-hour shifts back to back. Eventually the 58th Bomb Wing received its 175 B-29s and moved out to China to fly the first bombing raid on June 5, 1944, against a railroad facility in Bangkok, Thailand.

With production problems being solved and more B-29s available, the focus shifted to getting as many crews and planes into action as fast as possible. Sometimes, after a crew was trained, it was sent to a "staging" base. There, final processing was done before the crew and plane left for overseas. The major staging base for the B-29 was located near the town of Herington, Kansas. Herington is about 70 miles west of Topeka, and 26 miles south of Interstate 70. Population today is around 3,000, somewhat less than it was in 1940. The air field was located seven miles east and three miles north of Herington on 2,138 acres of flat Kansas prairie. It was planned as a satellite field of Topeka Army Air Field of the Second Air Force. Some important considerations in selecting Herington as a base site were the town's location as a rail center, very little fog, the land was flat and easy to build on, and it was an inland location. Construction began in September 1942 and was completed in April 1943. Originally intended as an interceptor base for P-38s, it was later changed to

An aerial view of Herington Army Air Field, circa 1944. USAF

A close-up view of the 406th Sub-Depot at Herington, circa 1944. Note building labels and B-17 and B-24 on the ramp. USAF

a processing base for B-24s. The processing of B-24 crews continued until June of 1944, when the base was prepared for the staging of B-29s.

Herington Army Air Field was big and some of it remains today. Walking across the 900-foot-wide, 3,000-foot-long concrete parking ramp, one can sense the presence of the B-24s, B-29s, and the men who left here long ago. Many never returned. Over 500 B-29s were lost in the war against Japan and about 60 percent of all B-29s that went overseas staged through Herington Army Air Field. The three 6,700-foot runways are still intact, as are two of the original three hangars. The roar of the Wright engines, each with 2,200 horsepower, is gone. It's been replaced by the whisper of the prairie wind across the open area where 317 buildings once stood. Today, only some foundations remain. The swimming pool, once the second largest in the state of Kansas, is now used as a target shooting range by a gun powder company located on the former air base.

The married personnel of the field lived off base, as did the dependents of the crews being processed. This put a tremendous strain on the town of Herington, and produced a boom economy. In effect, the population doubled due to the influx of personnel at the air field. However, the relationship between the town of Herington and the base personnel was excellent. The townspeople went out of their way to make the airman at home and the men from the base replied in kind. Dances were often held in one of the hangars and big-name bands were brought in. Shuttle buses would take the townspeople to the dances because they were always a big social event.

Housing space for dependents would have been virtually impossible to find had the people of Herington not opened their homes. Many converted their homes into apartments and rented the rooms for about $10 per week. They could have charged much more. The weekly rate was charged because the crews were here for about a week. The servicemen were delighted to have this one last chance to be with their wives and sweethearts. A housing committee was set up to keep track of available rooms and, when necessary, to help airmen find space. This was particularly helpful because sometimes parents would come, as did wives, and girlfriends. Once a rental rate was set it was not allowed to be changed. Mark Mills writes about the processed B-29 aircrews leaving the field. "So there was a plea to all in Herington to open their homes to the men and their wives in order for them to be together. When the men left in the morning they never knew whether they would be home that evening, and they would generally set up a system to let their wives know they were flying to the Pacific Area like, 'I don't like coffee for supper' or 'What are you having for lunch?', etc. Then the wives would stand out in the yard to await their husbands' planes flying overhead. The pilot would slightly dip the wings and the wives would wave white tea-towels at them. Some never returned." Forrest Clark was stationed at Herington and remembers it differently than some others, he writes, "I was stationed at Herington Air Base, Kansas, in August and early September 1943 when our crew assembled there for pre-overseas training and assignment. There was nothing around the base but wide-open Kansas prairie 50 years ago. The town itself was small and without major attractions for airmen who were about to go into combat zones and perhaps not come back. We were sweating out going either to the Pacific war zone or to the European combat zone. It was excessively hot as only a Kansas summer can be . . . When it came time for us to take off we had to wait until we were airborne to open our orders to discover where we were heading. I will not forget Herington base for another reason. There had been some crashes of military aircraft from the base and therefore flight crews were very uptight. I recall that at the supply hut and parachute shop the sergeant in charge would hand over chutes to new flight crews, look at them carefully to see if they were inspected, and say, 'Okay, this is a regulation packed parachute. But if for any reason it doesn't work you may bring it back and get another.' Then he would laugh so that all the crew members could hear. At Herington airbase there were no crowds to see us off, no girlfriends, no family, no bands or ceremonies. It was a lonely period and as we looked back after clearing the runway we all said we hoped we would never see Herington airbase again."

Many townspeople volunteered their time to make the airmen's stay more pleasant. This included inviting them into their homes for a Sunday dinner, and working at the local USO Club, located downtown at Broadway and Main. The USO became a community center where the men would meet their wives or girlfriends when they were off duty. There were Bingo games, a dance floor, places to make sound recordings to send home, space to write, make telephone calls, or just talk. There was also a snack bar, and the prices were less than what was charged in the local restaurants. The snack bar was not allowed to make a profit. Any surplus was used to entertain the serviceman. Often, this was done by

The former Herington Army Air Field while being used as a Beech Aircraft Corp. production facility for the conversion of C-45s, circa 1954. There are about 145 planes sitting on the ramp area. The hangar at the top of the photo and the one at the bottom have been refurbished and remain today. The second hangar from the top of the picture no longer exists, only its foundations remain. The third hangar from the picture's top was the Weights and Balances hangar and it was destroyed by fire.

A 1960's view of the former air field after most of the buildings were removed.

The Herington Army Air Field swimming pool circa 1944. The pool was dug with hand tools by civilian and military volunteers. At one time, it was the second largest swimming pool in the state of Kansas. It is 75' wide and 200' long.

The former Herington AAF swimming pool, as it was in 1995. The pool is now used as a shooting range for a powder company to test their products.

. . .

One of the two remaining hangars as it appears today. This was the South hangar.

The Weights and Balances hangar as it was in 1987. Here equipment, cargo etc. was weighed prior to being placed aboard the aircraft. THOLE

Part of the 900' wide, 3,500' long parking ramp in front of the hangars. Normally there were 50–60 B-29s parked here while the crews and planes were being processed for overseas. This is how it appeared in 1995.

The North Hangar, as it appeared in 1995. It is one of two hangars still existing. It has since been extensively refurbished. In the foreground are the remains of another large hangar.

Interior view of the North Hangar.

Remains of a bomb sight storage vault, located near the South Hangar. Here the secret
Norden bomb sights were stored and kept under 24 hour guard when not in use.

. . .

giving away free telephone calls home.

The war was very good for Herington businesses. People made money—lots of it. But often, they were not proud of it. One resident wrote, "And, Oh!, our stores were—I hate to say it, but everybody understands that war makes business. And Herington was just as busy in every business. Every business house in Herington prospered. You know, everybody prospered. It's too bad we have to profit during the war, but we do." So Herington was busy during this time, not only making money but also volunteering time and effort. People made cookies and cakes for the USO and for the many troop trains that stopped in Herington on their way elsewhere.

Many people of Herington became very close to the servicemen and their families due to the volunteer work, and when the crews left they felt as if they had lost a member of their family. Floyd and Marjorie Barnes remember these times well. Mr. Barnes enlisted in November 1942, and arrived at the field while it was still under construction. The runways were in and the hangars were finished, but that was about it. Early arrivals got their food and billeting supplies from Ft. Riley, Kansas, and slept where they could find space, usually in one of the hangars. Mr. Barnes distinctly remembers the Field Artillery rations from Ft. Riley and they're not fond memories. He originally was at the field simply to be processed through in a B-24, and continue overseas. However, his orders were changed and he remained at Herington until the field closed in October of 1945. Marjorie lived in the nearby town of Delavan and worked in Sub-Depot supply. She and Floyd met in Herington and were married at the base chapel. Mr. Barnes was the First Sergeant of the 47th Aerodrome Squadron, and recalls that the processing of the B-24 crews was fairly straightforward. It took about 5-10 days, and its purpose was to join the fully trained crews with a new B-24 and prepare them for overseas movement. There were several parts to the program. First, the ever-present paperwork had to be updated. This included personnel records, orders, bringing back pay up to date, and making out a will. The preparing of the final will often produced a lonely feeling and made the war seem very real. Physicals were given, clothing was inspected and issued, along with other items of equipment. The aircraft was assigned, checked out, and flight tested. Crews were given a prisoner of war lecture, and briefed concerning the routes to be traveled (within the United States). Final destination was in a sealed envelope and this was normally opened after leaving the final fuel stop to

overseas. The last thing was the schedule for departure to the Port of Embarkation.

Herington was a B-24 staging field for 11 months before switching to B-29s. Many famous B-24s passed through here including the "Lady Be Good," "Sad Sack," "Wee Willie," "Feather Merchant," "Thunder Mug," and "Snafu." During April 1944, the 492nd, 489th and 491st Heavy Bomb Groups were processed. With the conversion of the field to B-29s the pace quickened, and the field's peak activity was reached. This occurred in late 1944, when 2,300 officers, enlisted men and women were assigned. Including the number of B-29s' crews being processed, the total exceeded 3,000.

Early processing of B-29s crews, presented problems not faced with the "Liberators." There were no modifications done at Herington, but it did become an unofficial training base. Many crews arrived at the field with extremely limited training in an actual B-29. Early on, there simply were not enough B-29s for training, so much of the training was done in B-17s or other aircraft. As a result, the early crews stayed for as long as a month, learning how to handle their complex aircraft. Often, they left on training flights and did not return until the next day. Of course, minor problems with the planes had to be fixed, and this often kept the maintenance personnel working 24 hours a day, replacing faulty equipment, and handling the aircraft commander's "squawk" sheets. A typical month saw 86 crews and 76 aircraft processed. Often, base personnel were required to work around the clock, and with this effort often processed 240 crews in a month.

In command of the field during the B-29 processing, was Major Henry Dittman. He was extremely well liked and respected by the base personnel. Lt. Quinton L. Burgess was assigned as a Section Head in the Armament Section and remembers Major Dittman as a "tobacco chewing, pile driving" officer who made full Colonel at the old age of 29. During this time, Herington Army Air Field received the Meritorious Service Unit Plaque. Herington was the first field in the Second Air Force to receive a rating of "superior" on an Annual General Inspection. Colonel Dittman left Herington in September of 1945 to assume command of Kearney Army Air Field. Later, he became Commandant of Cadets at Texas A&M. He died in August of 1980.

Many famous commanders and their crews were processed at Herington, including Generals Curtiss Le May and Emmett O'Donnell. Col. Beirne Lay, Jr. (author of *Twelve O'clock High!*) also passed through

Building remains located just inside the entrance to Herington Army Air Field. In this area was located the Theater, Post Exchange (PX) and Bowling Alley. Off in the distance is the field's water tower. It had a 100,000 gallon capacity.

Today's view of the Community Buildings. The structures on the left also came from Herington Army Air Field.

After the war, some of buildings were moved from the field into the town and used for various purposes. This picture shows a former air base building in the background with another foundation being prepared. The buildings have been updated and are still used today. The foundation shown is for the Community Building. It is used for dances, graduations, auctions, weddings, etc.

. . .

here. Most crews left with the aircraft assigned to them when they arrived at Herington; however, some were flown by the Air Transport Command or traveled by train to a Port of Embarkation. The airplanes originally came to the field from modification centers and were flown in by Air Force Ferry personnel.

The last Wichita-built B-29 left the factory on a bright sunny day in October of 1945 and it wasn't long afterwards that Herington was shut down. This occurred on November 14, 1945. The base sat idle for a while, during which time the War Assets Administration sold much of the equipment and many buildings. Some barracks were moved to the city of Herington to create a fairground, and others are still there today. The base hospital's wards, surgical wing, and nurses quarters were used to replace Herington's original hospital. They served this purpose until a new hospital was built in 1973. The base chapel was moved to Latimer, Kansas, about eight miles away, and today it's the Zion Lutheran Church. In March of 1948, the city of Herington was given title to the field. This was near the time when the Air Force Academy was looking for a permanent location, so in January of 1950, the city made a formal proposal to the Site Selection Board for location of the Academy at Herington. In the early '50s the Beech Aircraft Corporation located a C-45 conversion production facility on the field, and stayed there until 1960.

Today, the field serves as the Herington Municipal Airport, and industrial park. It is maintained in excellent condition. The North-South runway has been resurfaced, and has an NDB approach. The water tower used during WW II, is 130 feet tall and is used as a mount for the field's rotating beacon. The water and sewage systems installed during the field's construction are still maintained and used today. The two remaining hangars have recently been refurbished and are in fine condition. If you are ever near Herington, it is well worth your time to visit the field. The people of Herington are warm, friendly, and proud of their past. Most everyone has had a connection with the field or knows someone who did. They will be pleased to talk with you about it. Also, you may see artifacts from the field kept at the Tri-County Historical Museum in Herington.

Former Herington Airfield hospital buildings. Following the base's closing they were moved into the town where they again served as a hospital until the city built a new one.

The former base fire station, no longer in use.

PREPARING C-47s FOR WAR

Baer Field

IN THE EARLY morning of June 6, 1944, about 13,000 men of the 101st and 82nd Airborne Divisions were preparing to jump into the night sky over Normandy, France. They were carried by more than 800 planes, part of the largest airborne invasion ever. A little more than three months later, on September 17, more than 2,000 planes carrying troops, equipment and pulling gliders were in the air on an even larger airborne assault—Operation Market Garden, the invasion of Holland. The 440th, 441st, and 442nd Troop Carrier Groups were at Normandy via Baer Field, Indiana. Probably more than half of all C-47s used in these major airborne operations had their final flight test at Baer Field. In fact, more C-47s were final flight tested at Baer Field than at any other airfield in the United States. This was the last stop prior to leaving for overseas. Baer Field also processed aircrew and airplanes of the first three Army Air Forces B-26 groups to operate the aircraft in the North African and Mediterranean theaters of operations. And for a short time, the 31st pursuit group was here prior to the beginning of the war. The people at Baer Field made a major contribution, one that is not well known. It was important to the role played by the Army Air Forces during World War II.

Baer Field is located about seven miles southwest of Fort Wayne, Indiana, between State Highways 1 and 3. Fort Wayne was often called "Fort Rain-Windiana" by the pilots stationed there because it was often either raining or windy. The field is named after Paul Baer, a Fort Wayne native, born in 1894. A 16-victory ace, he flew with the Lafayette Escadrille and the 103rd Aero Squadron AEF Air Service during World War I and was awarded the Distinguished Service Cross, the Legion of Honor, and the Croix de Guerre. He continued to fly after the war, opening air mail routes in South America, and participating in many aviation experiments. He died on December 9, 1930, while flying mail and passengers, when his Loening C-2-H amphibian crashed on takeoff from Shanghai, China. He is buried in Fort Wayne.

Early in the war years, defense-related construction was going on at a feverish pace all over the United States and especially in Indiana. Baer Field escaped some of this because the airdrome was about completed prior to the start of the war. The field was unique in that its establishment at Fort Wayne was at the request of the city. The location for many airbases was often a decision made by the War Department with little input by the people affected. The citizens of Fort Wayne wanted the base, and the city took options to buy 700 acres for that purpose, should the War Department decide to build a field there. The decision to build at Fort Wayne came much quicker than expected. Early in January 1941, the War Department told the town that it would locate a base there if possession of the land could be had by February 1. That was less than 30 days away. It simply was not possible to handle the real estate and financial matters that quickly. However, the situation was saved by 30 businessmen, who signed notes totaling the needed $125,000. Then four of the local banks advanced the city that amount of money to buy the land. Land owners were told to be ready to vacate in 15 days. The government signed a $1 annual lease, and now the construction could begin.

Like most of the Army Air Forces sites in Indiana, the land was relatively easy on which to build. I. L. Griffin, a local contractor, had the contract to clear the land for $3,500. There were eight homes, seven barns, and some other buildings to be razed. Some parts were heavily timbered and the drainage caused problems that cost $180,000 to correct. The original plans called for approximately 700 acres and 83 buildings. During the war, the base continually expanded so that by the end it had over 1,000 acres and more than 250 buildings. There were three runways, each about 6,300 feet long.

During the initial phase of the field's construction, base headquarters was located on the second floor of the National Guard Armory on North Clinton Street. The first Commanding Officer, Major Eugine Lohman, and his staff of four were located in one room of the Armory. At this point, everything

Baer Field Headquarters building just before completion in February 1942. The building was on Ferguson Road and just across the street from today's terminal parking lot.

was spartan. Office furniture was a homemade desk with some typewriters and one bookcase. The filing cabinets were the window sills with rooks used to hold down the papers. Later, half of a ping-pong table was added along with several banquet tables from the Knights of Columbus meeting hall. Office supplies were donated by local office supply dealers. Many civilians were being interviewed for later employment at the field, but there were no female personnel inside the building. At that time, the Armory was being used for pre-induction physicals, and nude selectees were everywhere. So, female candidates for employment were interviewed at the flag pole in the front of the building.

The contract for runway construction was signed in February, and for the first hangar in April. The first troops to be housed on the base was a Quartermaster company commanded by 2nd Lt. Ewing Elliott. At this time, the roads and walks were nowhere near completion, and spring rains made them virtually impassable. Mud was everywhere. It seemed like there was more mud inside the buildings than was outside. Some enterprising GI put up this sign, "Please do not track the mud outside as there is enough there now." It would not be until the summer of 1942 that most roads were paved.

Construction was at a breakneck pace because of the rapid expansion of all defense related projects in 1941. The major part of the original building project was finished by July, about 150 days after the lease for the land was signed by the War Department. Concrete for the runways was laid starting in July at the rate of 6,500 cubic feet per day. By October, a small city had been built where only farmland had existed before. The field was complete with a chapel,

barracks, fire station, hospital, administration building, warehouses, mess halls, class rooms, and repair shops. More would be added later. The "official" first landing took place on the 11th of November; however, the first plane to land at Baer Field was probably flown in by 1st Lt. Horace E. Dimond in August 1941. Horace was flying a PT-17 out of nearby Smith Field, and recalls seeing the new field under construction. As was often the practice in those days, pilots were quick to take the opportunity to be the first to land at a new airfield. Sometimes, they would claim to be low on fuel or "lost." Horace made no such claim. He saw the new field and landed on the north-south taxiway, because the runways were still under construction. The Army took possession of the field on October 31, 1941. Col. Lohman, who had been with Baer from the beginning, was transferred soon after to Langley Field, Virginia. He would be followed by 14 other commanding officers before the field closed in 1947.

The construction of Baer Field, including later additions through March of 1944, cost over 10 million in 1940 dollars. The impact of this spending, plus other war related construction in Fort Wayne, had a significant impact on the economy. During April to September 1941, Indiana industrial plants were awarded 975 contracts totaling $607 million. This did not include sub-contracts or lend-lease materials. The influx of business raised employment and payrolls to record levels. Fort Wayne rapidly became a good place for business. At this time, the local newspapers were full of articles about Baer and other defense related activities. After the war started, there was little or no news of military happenings at the field. The *Fort Warne News Sentinel* of November

Aerial view of Baer Field in October 1942. SMITHSONIAN

Troop housing area during construction, May 1941. USAF VIA ROGER MYERS COLLECTION

Large hangar and control tower in 1941. Present-day terminal is in this location. USAF VIA ROGER MYERS COLLECTION

. . .

5, 1941, talked about the P-39s soon to be stationed there; they "travel at 400 mph."

Many companies ran "welcome" advertisements including the Keenan and Anthony Hotels, Columbia Liquors Co. and Wayne Hardware. Indiana Tech. offered courses in drafting, mathematics, etc., to be taken after work hours. This would help the worker avoid "the inevitable layoff" following the emergency. Mayor Harry W. Balls was quoted as saying: "Nothing left undone to guard against danger of sabotage." City policemen received special training in first-aid, the fire station was rehabilitated and streamlined, equipment was modernized, and personnel were given intensive training.

The Studebaker Corporation aviation engine plant was in the final stages of completion. It would employ 1,400 people on its 40-acre site. Studebaker would make B-17 engines among other things. General Electric ran an ad telling about the largest expansion program in its history. Twenty-eight building projects were in the works with a $40 million commitment, part paid by the government. G.E. had just received a multi-million dollar award to make turbosuperchargers. They would be built at a factory in Fort Wayne that had not yet been constructed. This open reporting of events soon changed. About a year later, the *News Sentinel* reported, "When airline planes fly over the city, all curtains must be drawn at least five minutes before reaching Fort Wayne and for five minutes after passing over. Curtains must remain drawn during landings and takeoffs. Only Army and regularly scheduled planes are permitted to fly over Fort Wayne."

As the field was nearing the completion of its first major construction phase, it was assigned to the First Air Force with headquarters at Mitchel Field, Long Island. The major responsibility of the First Air Force was the organization and training of bomber, fighter, and other units and crews for assignment overseas.

The 31st Pursuit Group, the first to be equipped with the P-39 Airacobra, was assigned to Baer Field. The group had been activated at Selfridge Field, Michigan, in February 1940. The group filtered into the field slowly with the balance arriving on December 6, 1941, following three months of training and maneuvers in Louisiana. The men were looking forward to some rest following their strenuous training over the past three months. Also many were from the State of Indiana and happy to be home. However, Japan attacked Pearl Harbor the next day. Part of the group left four days later and within weeks the entire group was gone. By May, they were in England where they would be equipped with Spitfires and assigned to the Eighth Air Force. They entered combat in August 1942. The 78th Fighter Group was activated at Baer Field in February 1942. The group originally served in England flying P-38s and later was transferred to the Twelfth Air Force for a short time serving in North Africa. The group returned to England in 1943 flying P-47s and later P-51s as part of the Eighth Air Force.

Baer Field was assigned to the Third Air Force in March 1942. In May 1942, a transient group (probably the 38th) of B-26 Marauders stopped for servicing while on their way to the West Coast. This group would later participate in the battle of Midway. The field was closed to air traffic during the late Spring and Summer of 1942 in order to prepare for its role

Bomb sight storage buildings in 1942. Typically the Norden Bomb Sight was kept in concrete and steel vaults inside these buildings and was under 24-hour guard.

USAF VIA ROGER MYERS COLLECTION

Lt. Horace E. Dimond flying past the control tower in his T-6. This was a publicity shot staged for the local newspaper, *The Journal Gazette*, taken in September 1941. Lt. Dimond was the first to land an aircraft at Baer Field. DIMOND

of processing aircrew and aircraft. Some of the changes made during this time was strengthening the runways, necessary to accommodate the increased weight of the B-26s, C-46s, C-47s, and building additional hangars. The roads were finally paved. While being used by the I Concentration Command, Baer Field staged and processed medium bombardment groups. The first tactical units started to arrive for processing in September 1942. Later on, the field was assigned to the I Troop Carrier Command. Then its responsibility was the processing of tactical units of the Troop Carrier Command.

Early in April 1942, Ed Shenk was employed at Baer Field. Later, he would become Foreman of Flight Test and work at the field until the end of the war. Ed recalls his arrival at Baer and, at that time, the only planes were two Boeing 247Ds (C-73s) sit-

ting on the ramp. There was little to do because at the time the field was being upgraded to handle its new mission. So, the challenge was to keep busy. He was constantly looking for something to do and often helped shovel cinders to pass the time. He also worked at the welding shop at night and became so skilled that he was almost transferred to this duty on a permanent basis. But Ed wanted to be a mechanic. Later in August, he and several others were sent to Alliance, Nebraska, to interview people for the Alliance Air Base, then under construction. Ed stayed there thirty days interviewing. He remembers lots of confusion, with events moving very fast. The interviewers simply took a person's word for his ability and hired on that basis. When Ed returned to Baer in September the situation had changed. The field was covered with B-26s and everything was in full operation.

Most of the planes and crews were processed at Baer after transfer of the base to the I Troop Carrier Command. The mission of I Troop Carrier Command was to fly troops with their equipment into combat areas. They also flew wounded from the area of combat to hospitals. Baer's responsibility was the processing of Troop Carrier Command units for the I Troop Carrier Command. Planes and crews were joined at Baer and from there went directly overseas. Some of the major parts of the crew/plane joining tasks were:

1) Receiving and classifying personnel assigned to the I Troop Carrier Command.

2) Making sure the personnel records were up to date.

3) Handling basic training, i.e., range firing, instruction on flight techniques, Link training time, and an endless number of briefings on the war zone to which the crews were going.

4) Physical examinations, that included dental work. It might be a long time before the person leaving Baer would see a dentist, so considerable attention was paid to the teeth. The dental clinic was kept busy. During a 35-month period, there were almost 64,000 examinations, with over 40,000 fillings and about 9,000 teeth removed. Almost 1,000 dentures were fitted.

5) Supplies and equipment were issued. This varied from bicycles, to C-rations, to first-aid jungle kits, to screwdrivers. Since, the planes and crews were going directly overseas from Baer, anything the crew thought they might need was jammed aboard the aircraft. This was especially true if they were being sent to a field in an isolated area. Some equipment was not available in time for the planes departure overseas, so it was bought locally. For example, 2,100 fly fishing puff balls and streamers were purchased for $525.80 and were packed into jungle kits. Fifteen thousand feet of water hose costing $4,440.50 was bought to comply with the directive requiring 50 feet on each C-47. Five hundred crew chief ladders were also bought in Fort Wayne at a cost of $3,745. One ladder was placed on each plane.

6) All equipment, including the aircraft, received a final check.

Here's how a C-47 was typically checked out at Baer Field. After the plane's manufacture it was flown to a modification center. At the center the plane was updated according to the latest modification orders and received the necessary equipment and changes to suit it for its final destination. From the modifica-

tion center the C-47 was flown to Baer Field. Baer's responsibility was to inspect the aircraft and make any appropriate final changes; i.e., install long-range fuel tanks, remove unnecessary equipment, and give it a final flight test. After the final flight test, the ship was turned over to its crew. Baer's inspection of the C-47 was very detailed and involved considerable maintenance, repair, and modification. There were two stages. The first was an assembly-line type of operation in the largest hangar where everything was checked. Examples of some of the problems found were leakage of hydraulic fittings, generators not working, loose electrical fittings, instruments inoperative, low fluid levels, and missing parts, especially clocks. One C-46 arrived with a block of wood in the carburetor air filter.

Long-range fuel tanks were installed in the fuselage. If the plane was going to England, it received two 100-gallon tanks, Africa required four 100-gallon tanks, and if the Pacific was its destination, then eight 100-gallon tanks were installed. Extra oil was also required and this was put into a 50-gallon drum in the fuselage with a hose to each engine through the wing. When the oil level got low, more would be hand pumped from the drum to the engine's oil tank.

The second stage was the last inspection. Here the plane was flight tested and then turned over to its crew. Ed Shenk, as Foreman of Flight Test, and his crew of eight civilian mechanics would pre-flight the planes. The engines were run up, the plane taxied and then flown by military crews to check instruments, radios and single engine operation. The planes were flown north from Baer to Kendallville, Indiana, and back to Baer. This was about 80 miles round-trip. Around Kendallville, one engine was shut down to check how the aircraft handled. The military flew the planes during the flight test, but often the pilot would be accompanied by Ed or one of his crew. When the flight turned up additional problems, they were corrected by the Flight Test section.

Things moved very fast, as people learned their jobs by doing them. There were Pratt and Whitney technical people on the field, as well as other factory representatives. At one time, Ed counted 375 planes at Baer being prepared to go overseas. They were parked everywhere. Two of the three runways were closed because planes were parked on them. The hardstands were also packed with C-47s. Ed remembers one officer being upset with him because the planes were blocking a fireplug. Ed mentioned that since there were no shelves to put the planes on, they would probably have to stay where they were.

Ferguson road looking east, December 1942. Ferguson Road divided the building area from the flight line.
USAF VIA ROGER MYERS COLLECTION

One maintenance report totaled the number of planes processed at Baer from its opening through March of 1944. The total was 4,058 aircraft, which included 3,155 C-47s. March 1944 was a "typical" month, when 457 planes were serviced and departed overseas. At this time, there was an average of 520 officers, 2,874 enlisted personnel, and 986 civilians employees at the field.

While the planes were being serviced and made ready for overseas movement, personnel for these planes were also being processed. Jim Ross arrived at Baer in the fall of 1944, and stayed until April 1946. Originally ordered to be processed for overseas, his orders were changed and he was assigned as Asst. Operations Officer. Later he would become Operations Officer and then Base Engineer following the war. Jim recalls the pilots, co-pilots and crew chiefs being assigned as a crew for each C-47. In some cases, a navigator was assigned, depending upon the ship's destination. The process typically took about 2-3

weeks. Paperwork was handled, equipment issued, and some training accomplished. His staff would process between 10-40 crews per day.

Early in the war, a lot of training was very brief or non-existent. This was particularly true where men and machines were rushed into combat to meet an enemy that had been preparing and fighting for years. Our young men and women would pay dearly because of the political indifference and starvation budgets for military preparation prior to Pearl Harbor. This low level of training and experience was also true for crew chiefs. Ed Shenk remembers putting together a two-week course for crew chiefs who had never been to any crew chief school or, in some cases, had never been inside an airplane. About the best he and his men were able to do was teach them how to start the engines, taxi the aircraft, and drain water from the sumps. From there, they went overseas. This would change. Training films were first used at Baer in June 1942 and by August 1943, there were 165 training films; later on, this would grow to 485 films, and numerous other training aids.

In addition to processing new aircraft, Baer repaired and refurbished "war wearies." Lt. Gordon Baldry was a test pilot in the summer of 1944, and recalls testing one C-47—"Catfish." This was the same plane that he had flown for nine months in the Solomon Islands. She had served him well on the flights between New Caledonia and Guadalcanal, and now was back at Baer for repair and reassignment.

USO tours often entertained at the field with stars such as Judy Garland, Ray Charles, Gene Krupa, Sammy Kaye, and Guy Lombardo. Sometimes this took place in hangar no. 40, and other times outside on a stand built near one of the hangars. The shows were for the military. Civilians were not allowed to attend. One evening Ed and his crew were in the audience at a show and were asked to leave, so they left and went back to work. Since their responsibility was, among other things, testing of engines, soon several were roaring right next to the entertainers. From then on, no one bothered the Flight Test Section when they visited a show.

Baer continued as a staging base for the I Troop Carrier Command until early May 1945, when its mission changed. It now became an assembly station for redeployment of personnel from U.S. and Europe to the Pacific Theater. This new assignment was short lived, and on December 31, 1945, Baer Field was placed on inactive status. Baer's last assignment was an Army Air Forces separation base. This lasted until March 10, 1946. After this, the base was gradually closed. The general mess closed on January 10, 1946, the Finance Office on February 6, and the Post Exchange on May 29. By that time, the Post Exchange, which at one time had 126 employees, was now a combination office, sales store and cafeteria, all being operated by two employees. Equipment was transferred to other bases, put into storage or sold off in small lots. Some items were sold as salvage. An advertisement in the March 6, 1946 edition of the *News Sentinel* solicited bids for aluminum scrap, electric storage batteries, canteen cups, mess kits, rubber garden hose, rope, grinding wheels, and exposed x-ray film. On February 6, 1947, the base was declared surplus to the War Department, and the last civilian employee left on June 27, 1947.

Today Baer Field is the Fort Wayne International Airport. There is not much left to remind us of the field's proud service during World War II. Two of the original hangars are still here, however No. 39 is semi-abandoned and will probably be torn down in the near future. No. 40 remains in fine condition, being used by Federal Express. Some foundations can still be seen, along what was probably Ninth St. They are slowly being obscured by weeds and brush. Other foundations are located behind the Parker plant located on Piper Drive. Outside the entrance to the terminal building near the parking lot there is a large stone memorial set up to recognize the field's 50-year history. The field has grown considerably over the years and includes a first class terminal building and longer runways. Additionally, the field is home to a National Guard unit that flies the F-16.

Squadron hangar, building no. 40, as it appears in October 1994. Often USO shows were staged in this hangar. Stars such as Gene Krupa, Judy Garland and Ray Charles paid visits to the field to entertain the military personnel. THOLE.

Another squadron hangar
remaining at Baer Field.
This one is in poor condition
and is slated for demolition.
THOLE

This marker is located next
to today's terminal building.
It recognizes the 50th anniversary of the fields opening in 1941. THOLE

There is little left of the
hundreds of buildings here
during WW II. These
photos, taken in October
1994, show some remains
of building foundations.
THOLE

Interior view of C-47 with long-range tanks installed. The number of extra fuel tanks installed ranged from two to eight depending upon the aircraft's destination. Each tank held about 100 gallons. USAF

437TH Troop CARRIER Group
Attrition

BAER FIELD SUB-DEPOT FLIGHT TEST

DATE RECEIVED *11-4-44* LL=4   DATE DELIVERED *15-30*   TYPE & NO. 30736
             21;40

DATE	WORK ACCOMPLISHED	DATE	WORK ACCOMPLISHED
	PR. FLIGHT: Shenk TEST HOP: *1. Co Pilot Clock Out of Order* *2. R. Wing Heavy.* *Shenk*		WORK SHEET: 1. Change carb. R. eng. 2. No fuel pres. L. eng. 3. L. prop 2750 4. Cargo door bungee bad 5. Drain cabin tanks 6. R. eng. nose leak 7. L. eng. prop seal leak *REPAIRED* *Shenk*

Baer Field Sub-Depot Flight Test form listing work done on an aircraft during November 1944. This card was typical of the thousands kept by Ed Shenk and his crew for each aircraft that was processed thru Baer Field.

View of ''aircraft checkers'' preparing a C-47 to leave Baer Field. Note the equipment being loaded aboard the aircraft. The more remote and isolated the C-47's destination, the more equipment would be carried when leaving Baer Field. USAF

THE LUFTWAFFE INVADES INDIANA

. . . .

Freeman Field

INDIANA CONTRIBUTED a large number of pilots and trained air crew to the USAAF during the Second World War. In fact, it played a major role with its four major training fields spread across the state. The first of the four was Baer Field located near Fort Wayne. For the most part, it served as a staging field for the I Troop Carrier Command. Another Army Air Field was Stout Field located near Indianapolis and was headquarters for I Troop Carrier Command. The third field was Atterbury Army Air Field situated just outside Columbus, Indiana. It had several roles during the war. The most important were, 1) a receiving base for the sick and wounded being transported to local military hospitals (Wakeman General—just a few miles away) and, 2) the training of glider pilots for the I Troop Carrier Command. Freeman Field was the fourth major training field. Freeman Field was a twin engined advanced training school during the war and quite something else afterwards. Freeman stands out from many of the other training fields because of its role after the war. The story is fascinating and somewhat forgotten.

Today Freeman Field is quiet. Where the 413 buildings once stood there is now a growing industrial park. The roar of the more than 200 AT-10 "Wichitas" has long since faded, replaced by the occasional sound of a small private plane using one of its still existing three runways. Corn and soybeans grow where once young aviation cadets struggled to master the art of navigation and instrument flying. Now, business buildings sit on the parade ground, formerly the scene of weekly parades by the 500 aviation cadets. A lone smokestack still stands in solitary tribute, it used to be part of the base hospital. The 600-foot-wide, 5,584-foot-long concrete parking apron is empty and weeds are growing through the cracks. Looking across its vast expanse, one can see corn growing in the mid-July heat. One large maintenance hangar is still here, but the five squadron hangars

are gone. However some foundations remain, and a new hangar has been built on the foundation of one squadron hangar. At this writing, the five former Link training buildings are still here and in good condition. Some buildings used during the war are in use; however, they are slowly being torn down and replaced by more modern facilities.

Freeman Field is located in Seymour, Indiana, about 60 miles south of Indianapolis. The field was named to honor Captain Richard S. Freeman, a 1930 graduate of West Point. Captain Freeman helped establish Ladd Field—today's Wainwright Army Base—just outside Fairbanks, Alaska. He was Ladd Field's first commander. Captain Freeman held the Distinguished Flying Cross, was awarded the Mackay trophy, and was one of the pioneers of the Army Air Mail Service. At the time of his death, he had 6,000 flying hours. Captain Freeman was killed on February 6, 1941, in the crash of a B-17 he was flying near Lovelock, Nevada. The aircraft was equipped with the then-secret Norden bomb sight, and had extensive equipment for cold weather flying. The B-17 was on its way to Wright Field when it exploded in mid-air. Sabotage was suspected, but never proven. Captain Freeman grew up in Winamac, Indiana, where he graduated from Winamac High School. He went to Notre Dame for one year prior to receiving an appointment to West Point. Captain Freeman died at age 33, and is buried in Winamac, Indiana.

Even by today's standards, Freeman Field was big. It consisted of 2,653 acres of flat to rolling farm land, with four runways, each 5,500 feet long, and contained about 413 buildings. At first, many of the farmers were reluctant to sell their land because it had been in the same families for generations. Also there was a fear that they would not receive a fair price. One family had just moved into a new six room Cape Cod home in April of 1942, only to see it torn down the following August. In the Spring of 1942, agreement was reached with the farmers being paid

Aerial view of Freeman Field circa 1946. At this time, the field was being used to store, refurbish, and fly former Luftwaffe aircraft. USAF

Freeman Field today. Two runways are still in use, and the former training area is being developed into an industrial park. Several buildings remain from World War II. LIZ

Main entrance to the field circa 1946 when it was involved in the evaluation of foreign aircraft. This was probably the North gate. USAF

an average of $150 per acre. The land was virtually free of obstacles. A small cemetery was moved, and a consolidated school closed. Construction began in May 1942, and on the cold, overcast morning of December 1, 1942, the field was activated. Work at this point was about 75 percent finished. The first significant number of enlisted men started to arrive by December 8, with the first cadets coming in on March 1, 1943. Flying training started the next day. The first flight was made by Aviation Cadet Arthur H. Cropsey, Jr. of class 43D. When training stopped in 1945, over 4,000 pilots had graduated the school.

Many of the officers and NCOs used to staff the field came from Napier Field, Dothan, Alabama, and Craig Field, Selma, Alabama. Other personnel were provided by Grange Field, Illinois, and Stuttgart Field, Arkansas. In addition, Camp Atterbury, Indiana, provided early support in the area of supply and messing. The first enlisted man on the field was Master Sgt. Claud Dorman, a mechanic who arrived from Craig Field on October 22, 1942. Colonel Runquist was the project officer prior to his assuming command. His prior assignment was Maxwell field, Alabama. Colonel Rundquist's aviation career started in 1918 when he took his initial flight training at Carruthers Field, Texas. He had many and varied assignments prior to his arrival at Freeman. Colonel Rundquist was an All-American football player at the University of Illinois in 1915-1918, and also loved to play tennis.

The decision to build at Seymour was made by the War Department without major input by the citizens of Seymour. There was a small airport in Seymour often visited by Col. Paul Preuss, who was native to the area. It is generally believed that he had some play in the decision to consider Seymour for the site. The selection was ideal. The town itself was served by a major railroad and had a good road network. The site was approved on May 21, 1942. Two major difficulties were faced during the construction of the field. One was poor weather conditions, the other being materials for the extension of the Pennsylvania Railroad onto the field. Because of the inclement weather, some parts of the runways were built under the cover of circus tents. Total cost of the field was 16 million dollars. Freeman Field was built for expansion. A 50 percent increase in electrical needs could have been met with existing equipment. This was also true for the water and sewage systems. The water reservoir has a 200,000-gallon capacity and is still in use today, as is the sewage system.

Freeman Field was a twin-engine advanced training school with many of its graduates moving on to combat via the B-17, B-24, B-25 and B-26. The Beechcraft AT-10 "Wichita" was the aircraft used for the training. This ship was unique in that it was built almost entirely of wood and was the first all wood craft to be accepted by the USAAF as an advanced trainer. There were 2,371 built and probably none exist today in flyable condition. The plane had side-by-side seating and full instrumentation, that included an automatic pilot. Powered by two 280-hp. Lycoming R-680 radial engines with constant speed props, it was relatively easy to fly. One interesting aspect of the Wichita was its wooden fuel tanks lined with a special synthetic rubber. Because of its wooden construction, furniture manufacturers and other woodworking companies were able to build major sub-assemblies.

In September 1944, the USAAF's first helicopter training school was established at Freeman Field. The helicopters used were Sikorsky R-4Bs and were flown direct from the Sikorsky plant in Bridgeport, Connecticut, to Freeman. This included a flight over the Allegheny mountains, quite daring for the time. The trip was 725 miles during which several records were set. One included the longest formation flight. The pilots were Major John Sanduski, and Lt. Norbert Guttenberger. These men, along with several others from Freeman, received their initial helicopter training at the Sikorsky plant.

Preparations for the arrival of the helicopters went on for several weeks before they were actually flown to Freeman. These preparations were kept under a strict lid of secrecy and the section assigned the preparation tasks was known officially as "Section B-O." Over time, these people were called the "Lifebouy Kids." This was due to the connection of the advertising phrase "B-O" with a deodorant soap named Lifebouy. At this time, helicopters were so new and revolutionary that people simply did not know what these strange looking craft were. The helicopter was first referred to as a "direct-lift" plane and considerable effort was made to insure that the word helicopter was pronounced correctly. However, the helicopter training program was short lived because in December 1944, it was transferred to Chanute Field, Rantoul, Illinois. Chanute Field was then under the Eastern Technical Training Command.

On June 14, 1945, General Orders No. 17 transferred Freeman Field from its old assignment as an advanced training base to the one which makes it truly unique in Air Force history. These orders were a direct result of a letter written by the Commanding General of the Army Air Forces, H. H. Arnold. It was his desire that a field be used as a repository and testing center for "enemy aeronautical equipment." In addition, all significant U.S. aircraft were to be obtained, stored, and preserved for an AAF museum at a site not yet determined. So at 11:59 PM, June 15, 1945, Freeman Field was placed under direct command of the Air Technical Service Command.

Several other fields were considered for this role. These included Wright Field in Dayton, Ohio, along with Clinton County Army Air Field in Wilmington, Ohio. Wright Field was involved in other projects, but Clinton County was given serious consideration. The field at that time was part of the Wright Field complex and used primarily for glider operations; however, considerable construction would have been needed. So, Clinton County was not used. In May, a group of officers from Wright Field visited Freeman to look over the facilities and make a complete inspection of the field. Their inspection showed the field would be ideal for use as a technical evaluation center and also for the safe keeping of U.S. aircraft. Early estimates of personnel required to fill the mission requirements were 74 officers and 705 enlisted personnel and/or civilians. Colonel Harvey C. Dorney was placed in command. Colonel Dorney was in the Engineering Division, Air Technical Service and was an exceptional pilot. He loved to fly the Me 108, and did so quite often. He also flew the Me 262 and even gave his wife a ride in one of the two seat models.

Freeman Field's mission was unique, and it was the only Army Air Force base with this kind of objective. Here's how its mission was stated, according to the base history—"Freeman Field was established with the mission of receiving, reconditioning, evaluating, and storing at least one each of every item of enemy aircraft material. This was to include items such as clothing and parachutes as well as the aircraft themselves. Also to be included were such items as anti-aircraft guns, radar, and similar devices. The field will also assemble and catalogue U.S. equipment for display at the present and for the future A.A.F. museum, the site to be determined at a later date."

Further mention of Freeman Field as a site for the storage and preservation of U.S. aircraft is contained in a teletype dated May 12, 1945. It said in part, "These will include one each of production models used by the A.A.F. during the war as well as earlier types dating back to the World War I and experimental types that never reached the production stage."

The story of this phase of Freeman Field's history is best told through the eyes of Mr. H. Ray White. At the time, the Air Force decided to establish a centralized location for their captured enemy aircraft at Freeman. Ray White was an Air Force Captain stationed at Wright Field. His job was to restore captured aircraft to airworthy condition for flight test and evaluation. Parts had to be fabricated for some aircraft. Inspections, preparation of flight instructions and sometimes major repairs were necessary. This required mechanical and engineering qualifications in addition to flight test duty. While at Wright Field, Ray was the Air Material Command's only Project Engineer Foreign Aircraft, and had been there since July 1943. Ray remembers this as "the most challenging position Wright Field had to offer."

When Captain White's inventory of enemy aircraft outgrew the allocated space at Wright Field, two hangars were rented for the project at the airbase in Vandalia, Ohio. Today, this is the site of the Dayton International Airport. Ray remembers on occasion, pilots from the Flight Test Section at the nearby Wright Field, would fly in to check out on an enemy aircraft. Some of the names he remembers included Russ Schleeh, Chuck Yeager, Don Gentile, and Dick Bong. He recalls that they were a good group, and only occasionally would he meet one who was over impressed with himself. Then, a quick ride in the Italian Macchi would be a good cure. The Macchi had a short wing to correct for torque, and the throttle worked backwards. Later when Freeman Field became the gathering point for the captured aircraft, he became Chief of the Flight Maintenance Branch at Freeman. Ray flew the first foreign aircraft to Freeman Field, a Junkers Ju 88.

Ray was an outstanding pilot and was considered one of best instrument pilots at Wright Field. Just to make things a bit more challenging, he would take all his instrument check flights with one engine out. If an aircraft could fly, Ray flew it. This included everything from the Me 262 to the B-29. Often, Ray's skilled feel for an airplane was required to save himself and the plane when problems developed during flight testing a reassembled aircraft. Mr. White remembers his first flight with the plane that would later become his favorite. It was almost his last. The aircraft a Bf-108 was a five-place, low-wing monoplane (painted red and orange) rumored to be the personal plane of Herman Goering, head of the Luftwaffe. The airplane had been reassembled

Main entrance today at the
North end of the field. THOLE

Former chapel at Freeman.
Later moved to Seymour
and is now the Trinity
Pentecostal Church. THOLE

The former Link trainer
buildings as they are today.
Their building numbers
were T-329 to T-333. THOLE

Former WAC mess hall, building no. 1054. THOLE

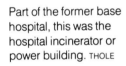

Part of the former base hospital, this was the hospital incinerator or power building. THOLE

This building located on the flight line was probably the crash shed. THOLE

. . .

Former maintenance building that may have been part of the sub-depot. THOLE

This building is being renovated and may be used as a museum to help preserve the history of the field. It was formerly an operations building located on the flight line. THOLE

The remains of a squadron hangar, and how it appeared in 1986 *(next page)*. THOLE

at Freeman Field; however, on the initial flight following reassembly, the cowl blew off while Ray was in the middle of his take off run. Ray braked to a stop, and taxied back down the runway, picked up the cowling, and returned to the Engineering Hangar. After the cowling was properly put on the plane, Ray took off again. This time the ailerons locked immediately after take off. He called the tower, reported the problem and explained that he would make a wide sweeping turn to line up with the runway. While approaching the runway, he lowered the wheels and immediately regained aileron control. After checking, it was learned that the hydraulic lines were installed on the wrong side of the landing gear struts, a condition that bound the aileron cables after the gear was retracted. Later, he was ordered to return the plane to Wright Field, which he did; however, he did not tell anyone the starting procedure. The ignition switch was a knot at the end of a cable.

Ray also had a mischievous streak. Once while working with the engineering section at Freeman Field, he was called by the engineering shop that had just finished an inspection of a British model of our C-45. Ray wasn't exactly friendly with the chief of engineering, so when asked to help solve a problem with the plane (it was on jacks in the hangar and the gear would not retract) his mischievous streak took over. Ray told the mechanics to flip the gear switch into the "up" position then "he would whisper into the plane's ear." He put one hand around the Pitot tube and blew into it. The wheels went up. He patted the plane on the nose and walked away. Only later did he explain the British system which helped pilots prevent retracting the gear before completely airborne.

At first both German and Japanese material were to be evaluated. However, in January 1946, this was changed and all Japanese equipment was to be sent to the Olmsted Field in Middletown, Pennsylvania. Three aircraft were retained at Freeman, a Nick 2, a Zeke and a Hamp.

When Freeman was transferred to the Air Technical Service Command, shipments of aircraft and associated material began to arrive at the field. Early on, the material came from Wright Field because there was a considerable quantity there which had not been evaluated. Much of the material had been in outside storage at Wright Field and was not in good condition. Lots of time and work was required to refurbish it. Meanwhile, considerable German aircraft and parts were being gathered in Europe, under the direction of Colonel Harold E. Watson. His story is fascinating and told very well in the book *Jet Planes of the Third Reich*, Monogram Aviation Publications, 1982.

Some of the first flyable examples of German aircraft arrived at Freeman Field on the British aircraft carrier *HMS Reaper*. The aircraft carrier docked at the port of Newark in late July 1945 after the planes had been prepared for overseas shipment and loaded at Cherbourg, France. Additional equipment, e.g., engines, wings, fuselages, etc., also arrived on the carrier and were shipped to Freeman by rail. Many problems had to be fixed before the planes could be flown. Engines had to be tested and fine tuned, leaks of all kinds fixed, and braking systems adjusted. Our people simply lacked the intimate knowledge of the German systems necessary to get maximum performance from the machines.

After considerable work, that took much longer

than anticipated, the planes were ready, and under the direction of Colonel Watson, were flown to Freeman Field. Perfect flying conditions were required because the planes still had German radio and navigational equipment. As the planes flew west, they were met with incredible surprise by the people who first saw them. It was the first time that many persons outside of the military had ever heard or seen a jet. Most people simply did not know what they were. Some of the aircraft that were delivered by the Reaper were Me 262s, an Ar 234 (a two-engined jet reconnaissance bomber), He 162s (a single engine jet fighter named by the Germans as the "Volksjager" or "People's Fighter"), and the Me 163 (a rocket interceptor). Later on in August, Colonel Watson flew a Junkers 290 into Freeman Field. The Ju 290 was a reconnaissance aircraft about the size of our B-29 and powered by four piston engines of 1,600 hp. each. It was captured near Munich, had a maximum speed of 270 mph, and range of 3,800 miles.

After the arrival of planes and equipment from the "Reaper" the evaluation program swung into high gear. By necessity, the evaluation was on a broad scale basis and specific work was done at Wright Field and in some cases Muroc Dry Lake (Edwards Air Force Base). The early estimates of 75 officers and 705 enlisted men/civilians to help conduct the evaluations was never reached. There were several reasons for this but principally, with the war in Europe over, many of the people assigned to Freeman were discharged after a brief stay. As a result, the personnel situation was constantly changing. For example, the post had four Sergeant Majors during September-December 1945. Replacements, when available, had less experience than their predecessors and most positions required highly technical skills.

Additionally, it was difficult to hire quality civilian help because the job was short term, severe housing problems existed, and the civilian personnel budget was cut. Many key projects were simply put aside and never done. Despite these drawbacks, considerable flying was done. For the first six months of operation, there were approximately 1,800 flights, both local and cross country, in U.S. and foreign aircraft. The only pilots who regularly flew the captured aircraft were Colonel Dorney, Captain Ray White, Lieutenant Holt (one of Watsons original group of pilots) and one other pilot, killed in a crash of a FW 190. Only once was Ray requested to do a flight test program, and that was on a Japanese Zeke. Ray also recalls doing some work with an Italian Macchi, but

that was about it.

This continued until V-J Day when Freeman's primary mission changed. Less emphasis was put upon evaluation, and more upon the display of the aircraft and equipment at various exhibits and air shows across the country. For example, in July 1946, Lt. Kenneth Holt flew an Me 262 to an air show held at Omaha, Nebraska. He made three stops en route.

It was not until September 1945 that the general public was informed of the existence of the collection of German aircraft. At that time the field was thrown open for the media. Reporters converged onto the field from across the country and the aircraft, along with other captured equipment, received national attention. Many of the aircraft were flown including the FW 190, Me 262, Ju 88, Ju 388, and the Hs 129.

Despite this press coverage and subsequent times when Freeman held "Open House," many citizens of Seymour were not aware of its activities. I recall talking with a local salvage dealer who, at the closing of Freeman, sold much of its equipment for scrap. He recalls one particular piece shaped like a ball, probably made of stainless steel. I mentioned to him that it could have been a fuel tank from a V-2 rocket. He was quite sure it was not because he thought no V-2 rockets were ever at Freeman. But they were. There were at least 25 different German aircraft at Freeman Field including the V-1 flying bomb.

The field also collected 71 different types of U.S. aircraft. These were later transferred to Davis-Monthan Air Force Base in Arizona, Wright Field, and the Douglas Plant in Chicago. The list included many aircraft still seen today, such as the P-38, P-47, P-51, B-17, etc., and others which are extremely rare or no longer exist. These included the XP-47H, YP-61, Fisher XP-75, B-32, XP-55, P-59, XO-60, and the O-47. There were several gliders: the XCG-14, XCG-15, XPG-2a, and XCG-16. The last three were towed by air to Orchard Place Airport (today's O'Hare Field in Chicago). The B-32 (42-108474) was stored at Davis Monthan for intended use at the Air Force Museum. However, it was scrapped.

So over the next several months the field was gradually shut down. Headlines from the *Seymour Weekly Republican* reported the steady demise of the field. On August 1, 1946, the paper reported that 101 buildings were taken over by the Public Housing Administration for transfer to Terre Haute, and Angola, Indiana. On August 29, headlines read "Freeman Field Announces Sale," in which 900 iron fence posts and 15,000 feet of barbed wire were to be sold as

Fisher XP-75 on display at
Freeman Field pictured are
Mrs. Bel Cramer and friend.
CRAMER

V-2 rocket with the field's
control tower in the
background. This photo
was probably taken at a
public showing of the field's
aircraft in September 1945.
Most of the field's aircraft
were on display at this time.
WHITE

Line up of foreign aircraft at
Freeman circa 1946. Note
the two Bf-108s. WHITE

Captain White standing next to his favorite plane, the Bf-108. This was rumored to be Herman Goering's personal aircraft. It arrived on the field in crates painted in the gaudy orange and yellow colors. WHITE

Heinkel He 162 A Salamander on display at Freeman Field. This was an attempt by the Luftwaffe to build a simple, easy to fly fighter. About 120 were produced but were too late to have any impact on the aerial war. Top speed was about 500 mph. WHITE

The Arado Ar 234B Blitz (Lightning). This aircraft was far ahead of its time, and if produced in quantity could have been a serious threat because of its speed, about 460 mph, and bomb load. WHITE

. . .

The Focke Wulf 190, one of the outstanding fighters of World War II. Note the squadron hangar in the background. WHITE

A good photo of a Junkers Ju 88, one of the most numerous and versatile aircraft of World War II. WHITE

surplus. On September 16, headlines announced "Scrap Lumber To Be Sold At Field" for $2 per pickup truckload.

On October 3, 1946, the paper reported "Freeman Field To Be Excess In 30 Days," and on October 17, "The Beginning Of the Deactivation Process." Finally on April 3, 1947, the newspaper announced, "Freeman Field To Be Disposed Of By April 30th."

So Freeman Field passed into history. During its training days over 4,000 pilots earned their silver wings, flying about 380,000 hours and logging in excess of 55 million miles. Its contribution was felt worldwide. Its work as an aircraft storage and refurbishing center was unique in Air Force history. Many of the planes found in museums across the United States were stored at Freeman. Thanks in large part to the vision of General Arnold, and the efforts of Freeman Field personnel, these planes still exist.

Following the war, Freeman Field like so many other training bases, became surplus. Over time, it slowly evolved into an industrial park that maintained its airfield to help attract industry. Rumors persisted about German aircraft and other equipment buried at the field prior to its closing in 1947. During the research of the history of Freeman Field, the author met with people familiar with the field's history, many of whom have been aware of the rumors for years. Additionally, two men were located who claimed to have been involved in the burying of equipment, one as a witness, the other as the operator of a bulldozer used to cover the trenches where surplus material was buried.

Dumping surplus material into pits and burying it was a common practice at war's end. The government tried to sell and/or give away the billions of dollars worth of military material after the war. This included everything from buildings, planes, mountains of parts, engines, and the everyday items found at the training bases. Think of a small city and all that's in it. The USAAF had hundreds of these small cities that were surplus virtually overnight, and now had to be disposed of. There were no funds available to maintain these bases, nor was there much desire to do anything but forget the war and move onto a peace time footing as soon as possible. So, the Air Force, along with the other services, moved quickly to discard this excess material. Ads appeared in newspapers, offering everything from aircraft to fencing to typewriters, at give-away pricing. Huge quantities of surplus material were sold to dealers and individuals, and some of it given away to schools and local governments. Thousands of aircraft were melted down into aluminum ingots, some were brand new, right off the assembly line. A lot of material not sold, given away, or scrapped was dumped into trenches and buried. The rumors of buried equipment persists at many of the former training fields this author has visited.

Freeman Field was special because of the unique nature of its mission late in the war. Not only were there more than a hundred German and Allied aircraft at the field, there were also warehouses filled with every kind of Luftwaffe equipment. General Arnold's orders establishing Freeman Field as the test center also stated he wanted at least one example of every kind of enemy equipment. This included radars, instruments, manuals, parachutes, binoculars, etc. Wright Field cataloged this material and retains the file in their archives. Correspondence kept on file at the Smithsonian between Wright Field and Freeman Field also confirm the existence of vast quantities of this German equipment.

Attempts have been made to recover the material rumored to be buried at Freeman. Its value to historians, museums, and aviation enthusiasts worldwide is impossible to calculate; however, the sandy soil and high water table existing at Freeman made the project extremely difficult. To date, no foreign material has been recovered, so the questions remain and the mystery continues.

TROOP CARRIER COMMAND

Stout Field Army Air Base

STOUT FIELD Army Air Base was a small field that played a big part in World War II. In terms of size, the aerodrome was modest, especially when compared with many other of the 700-plus Army Air Force installations existing during the Second World War. For example, Stout Field contained 357 acres, had about 130 buildings and four runways, the longest being 4,495 feet. Compare this with Buckingham Army Air Field, a flexible gunnery training center located east of Ft. Myers, Florida. That field had over 65,000 acres.

Stout Field had two key functions. The first was its responsibility as headquarters for I Troop Carrier Command and, as such, directed glider training activity at the other training bases throughout the United States. In addition, Stout Field was a training base. The training done there included, C-47 pilot transition, glider pilot training, and glider ferrying. Also, there were special projects, one of which included transferring aircrews and planes to the northwest coast during April/June of 1945. This project was called "Firefly" and its function was to patrol the forest areas of the region to report fires, some of which were expected to be caused by Japanese incendiary balloons.

Stout Field lies on the southwest edge of Indianapolis, just off Interstate 70 on Holt Road, about three miles from Indianapolis International Airport. Stout's history stretches back to 1926, when the city decided to open a municipal airport on 200 acres under the control of the 113th Observation Squadron, Indiana National Guard. It was named to honor Lt. Richard H. Stout, a pilot of the 113th Observation Squadron, who was born in Indianapolis, Indiana, on October 15, 1898, and enlisted in the French Army before the U.S. entry in World War I. He originally served as a driver in the Ambulance Service and was awarded the Croix de Guerre with gold, silver, and bronze stars for his bravery under fire. Later, he enlisted in the aviation branch of the Signal Corps. Following the war, he was commissioned in the Air Service Officer's Reserve Corps, before joining the Indiana National Guard in 1926.

He was killed in the crash of his plane on Schoen Field at Fort Harrison, Indiana, on October 3, 1926, and was buried in Crown Hill Cemetery, Indianapolis.

Stout Field was taken over by the state after the city relocated its airport three miles to the west. At this time there were few buildings and no paved runways. However, in 1931, the state allocated $45,000 for improvements. Later in 1940, a WPA grant of about $1,249,000 was announced for additional improvements. Runways were to be built along with two additional hangars, a control tower, and an administration building. Field lights were added along with locker rooms, showers, and recreation rooms. There were no barracks since this was a National Guard field and the men of the observation squadron did not live on base. A local newspaper commented at the time, "conversion at Stout Field from a 'grass' airport into a modern field would make it one of the key military fields in the national defense system." However, Stout was soon vacant as the 113th Observation Squadron was federalized and left for Camp Shelby, Mississippi, in January 1941.

Though empty, work by up to 600 men continued on the field's runways and buildings. Many wondered what it would be used for. As late as December 6, 1941, an article in the *Indianapolis Star* stated, "Stout Field expansion is big mystery—work rushed but vague hints fail to disclose future of National Guard's Airport—undergoing a tremendous and an expensive program but nobody seems to know why." The questions were answered when on April 7, 1942, the Army Air Forces leased the field from the state for $1 a year. By then, Stout consisted of 259 acres, four hangars (one under construction), some other buildings, and 15,000 feet of concrete runways. Since the administration building and hangars had been under construction via a WPA grant, they were built for permanent use, unlike the temporary buildings being constructed at most military fields during this period. The buildings were very attractive art-deco design, and were made of brick.

The official history for this period comments that the construction program was "proceeding at a snail's

Control tower and head-
quarters building for Stout
Field. This was also the
administration head-
quarters for the First Troop
Carrier Command. The
building is virtually
unchanged from its
appearance in 1943. THOLE

Building foundation
remains in the former
cantonment area for Stout
Field. Following the war and
into the 1950s, the buildings
were used for public
housing. Today, only a few
foundations serve as a
reminder. THOLE

pace . . . personnel were difficult to secure because
Civil Service rates of pay were far below the prevail-
ing wage scales in the community, and the rapid expansion of war related industries were exhausting
the available supply of manpower." To help solve the
problem a post utility officer was assigned to the field
and the emergency hiring of more workers started.
First priority was housing for the troops. A tent city
was built on 15 acres acquired for this purpose. Housing the soldiers in tents was a temporary measure
until barracks could be built. Toward this end another 80 acres were purchased north of the field.
One hundred and twenty-one buildings were authorized for construction, 43 of which were barracks.
They were completed just before Christmas 1942,
with the men moving in on December 23.

After the war, with the desperate housing shor-

tage that existed, the 80-acre site, that then contained
137 temporary buildings, was converted into civilian
housing. The area was named Tyndall Towne, and
the first families moved in during 1946. It was used
for housing until the early fifties when it was torn
down. The state purchased the land for $1,450.00.
Today, much of this area is open vacant land containing the foundations and other remains of the
Stout Field buildings. Five acres were used for an
Indiana National Guard building constructed in
1977.

To provide security for the rapidly expanding
base, a cyclone fence was built around much of the
aerodrome perimeter. The fence was loaned to the
field by the Indiana State Penal Prison at Pendleton,
Indiana. Sand bag emplacements were set up at important areas and the soldiers were armed with rifles

and Thompson submachine guns. This was late 1942 and there was still some concern about the possibility of an enemy airborne assault.

When the Army Air Forces took over Stout Field on April 7, 1942, there was virtually no U.S. military experience with gliders. The first large troop carrying glider, the CG-4A, would not be delivered until a year later in March 1943. Also, the first class of military glider pilots had not started their training until June 1941. This class consisted of 12 student glider pilots who were trained by civilian instructors; some were trained at Elmira, New York, and others at Lockport, Ill. The program expanded rapidly and by October 1943 there were 10,294 students involved in glider pilot training. Meanwhile, work was moving ahead on development of a large cargo carrying military glider. It had started during March 1941 when, at the direction of General Arnold, personnel at Wright Field began design studies of a military glider. This eventually led to a contract with Waco Aircraft Company that resulted in the CG-3A and, later, the larger and much more numerous CG-4A. Contracts to build the CG-4A were issued in July 1942, three months after the Army took control of Stout Field.

Like all other new Army air fields, Stout had start-up problems, one of which was the lack of experienced enlisted personnel. Most men had very little training, usually only eight to ten days basic. It was necessary to do most of the training outdoors because the classroom buildings were not complete. Poor weather caused much training to be canceled.

An aerial view of Stout Field today. Note how runways have been used as foundations for buildings. Clear area near top center of photo is former troop housing area. THOLE

. . .

This was in the late spring and early summer of 1942, only a few weeks after the Army took possession of the field. Facilities were very limited. Then, there were three squadrons on the field, Headquarters Squadron, Second Squadron, and the 38th Troop Carrier Squadron. Meals were served in a mess tent next to a hangar. It wasn't until January 1943 that the mess hall was opened in Building 158. By that time, the number of men being served at each meal had increased from 50 to 300.

One of the first arrivals at Stout was Bob Richards, a crew chief with the 38th Transport Squadron. Bob remembers the transition training of the new pilots, many of whom had served with the airlines and received a direct commission in the Army Air Forces. They were now at Stout to learn to fly "the Army Way." There was no cross-country training needed for these pilots. They primarily needed to practice "two point" or tail high landings. As civilian pilots their landings were "three point." The planes used had only recently been in the service of the airlines. They were former American, Eastern, and TWA ships all freshly painted olive drab on the outside, but their interiors retained the civilian seats, blankets, etc. According to Bob, the airplanes looked like they had just came in off a run.

As mentioned earlier, Stout Field was not only an active Army training field but also headquarters for I Troop Carrier Command. As such, Stout coordinated and directed training activities at other bases in the United States. While locations changed from time to time, some bases and their training activities were: Alliance Army Air Base (Alliance, Nebraska) troop training; Baer Field (Fort Wayne, Indiana) processing center for crews and planes bound for overseas; Bergstrom Field (Austin, Texas) radio school and some pilot training, also a combat crew replacement center; Bowman Field (Louisville, Kentucky) glider pilot training and air evacuation training; Lawson Field (near Ft. Benning, Georgia) here tactical units were trained and planes and crews provided for the nearby parachute school; Laurinburg-Maxton Army Air Base (Maxton, North Carolina) glider pilot training; and Sedalia Army Air Field (Warrensburg, Missouri), combat crew replacement center. Over time, some training centers were added and others dropped dependent upon the needs of the Army Air Forces. As an example, George Field, near Vincennes, Indiana, was later added, and used with Atterbury Army Air Field (Columbus, Indiana) for glider pilot training. Some other fields used were Pope Field (Fort Bragg, North Carolina), Malden

A CG-13 at Stout Field. This may have been the Ford YCG-13A that carried 30 troops; only one was made.
CRAMER

Students learning proper procedure to enter water during a class conducted at the nearby Westlake Park.
USAF

Army Air Field (Malden, Missouri), Blytheville Army Air Field (Blytheville, Arkansas), Marfa Army Air Field (Marfa, Texas), Scottsbluff Army Air Field (Scottsbluff, Texas), and Sturgis Army Air Field (Sturgis, Kentucky).

With the increase of flying activity at Stout, air control became a problem. The field was just three miles from the growing air traffic at Indianapolis Municipal Airport. It was not unusual for a commercial airliner to land at Stout by mistake. Due to the close proximity, pilots were often confused during their approach. Some pilots approaching one field would fly within the area controlled by the other. To help solve the problem, Stout's tower was moved from its location on the field to the top of the administration building and a new traffic con-

View from today's control tower looking at the two still existing hangars. The upper part of the tower is used for storage and still has a few of the field lighting controls remaining from WW II. THOLE

Picture taken from the former living area looking toward the control tower in the distance. THOLE

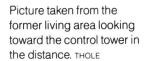

More remains of the former cantonment area. THOLE

Today's entrance to Stout Field. THOLE

trol system was put into effect. To help decrease congestion, Stout air traffic would be "stacked" at various altitudes and given their landing approach clearance by the tower. This did not end the confusion caused by the closeness of the two fields, but it did help speed the flow of Stout's traffic. The tower itself was the last word in modern convenience, being totally glass enclosed and air conditioned. It was installed in early February 1943 and the field was silent for just 58 minutes as control was transferred from the old to the new location. The tower saw considerable use. A flight operations report for 1944 showed that during the year 11,305 transient aircraft received cross-country clearances and approximately 16,000 aircraft were cleared. During the first quarter of 1945 there were 6,808 landings at Stout and 21,783 clearances.

Stout Field also had the rather unique distinction of having its control tower operate a traffic light. Bob Larsh remembers landing his B-25 on the field's runway that was very close to Holt Road. Because of its proximately to the road vehicular traffic was stopped when the B-25s landed and took off. A stop light was installed to do this and the light was controlled by the tower.

One of the more interesting activities at Stout was glider ferrying, during which gliders were air-towed from one base to another or from factories to the many Troop Carrier Command training bases. The glider factories included, Northwestern Aeronautical Corp. (Minneapolis, Minnesota), Robertson Aircraft Corp. (Kansas City, Missouri), and the G&A Aircraft Corp. (Willowgrove, Pennsylvania). The effort began on February 5, 1944, with three C-47s,

three power pilots, and one glider pilot. The first mission was to tow five gliders from Bowman Field, Louisville, Kentucky, to Pope Field, Fort Bragg, North Carolina. Soon after that, ten flight officer glider pilots were assigned for thirty days temporary duty and then replaced with glider pilots returning from tours in various theaters of operations. A typical glider ferrying operation would see a crew fly their C-47 tow ship to the glider factory where they would be met by a factory representative. Following a 30-minute test flight, they would tow the glider to its destination. After April 1944, gliders were generally towed two at a time. The number of gliders deliveries during this period averaged between 100-150 per month. There were 13 tow planes.

Early in 1944, Stout Field was involved in the testing of glider pick-up equipment used to "snatch" gliders into the air. Later in the year, a glider pick-up school was established at the field. The "snatch" system worked like this. Two poles resembling football goal posts were set up about 50 yards ahead of the glider that was to be picked up. One end of the nylon tow line was attached to the glider nose and the other end was hung between the two poles where it would be "snatched" by the hook of an arm extending from the tow plane, as it flew only a few feet from the ground. This technique was often used to retrieve gliders from almost inaccessible places. It was used following the invasion of Normandy and the invasion of Holland when it was critical to salvage as many CG-4As as possible, for further use. The technique also saved many lives when the glider would be loaded with wounded and "snatched" from locations where runways did not exist. One of its earliest

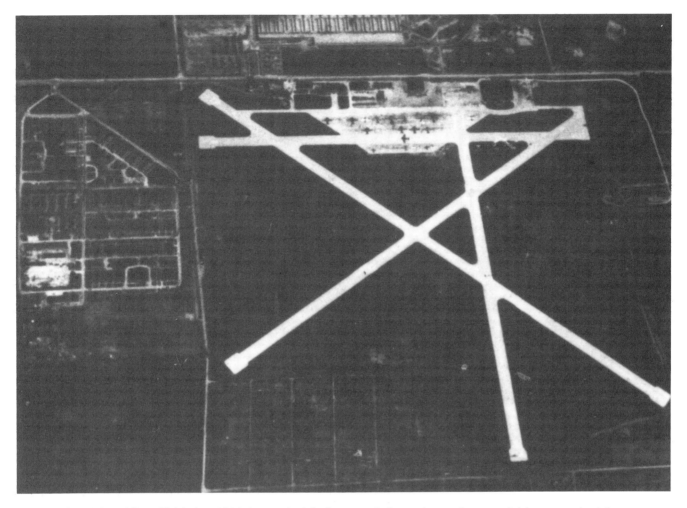

Aerial view of Stout Field, circa 1944. Area to the left of runways is the cantonment area containing approximately 137 buildings. USAF

combat uses was in Burma during April 1944.

Paul Cramer remembers the two glider "snatch" rides that he took. He recalls bracing himself for the sudden jerk "just like a parachute opening," when the tow rope stretched to its limit. Sometimes the plane would miss and then it would simply come around again for another try.

Glider pick-up crew training began at Stout Field in June 1944, following the transfer of this training from Maxton Army Air Base. The crew was made up of a pilot, co-pilot, radio operator, and a crew chief. The pilot was trained to place the plane in the proper position to make the pick up, the crew chief was trained to operate the pick up unit, and the co-pilot and radio operator were trained as assistants. Pilot training involved classroom and field work, including how to set up the pick up unit. Normally, they were given two demonstration rides, ten simulated and five actual pick ups with an empty glider, two pick ups with a loaded glider, and finally two solo pick ups. The course lasted about two weeks.

Starting in May 1944, Stout became a stopover point for sick and wounded troops being flown to stateside hospitals. Some had been flown from the European Theater in C-54s to Holleran General Hospital on Staten Island. They would then be flown to Stout and moved by ambulance to Billings General Hospital at Fort Harrison in Indianapolis. Others were transferred from one general hospital to another in the continental United States for specialized treatment. Many were sent to Wakeman General Hospital at Camp Atterbury, Indiana. Aircraft carrying wounded had top priority in traffic patterns. Other aircraft preparing to land or take off would be held to give first priority to air-evacuation planes.

An Open House was held at Stout Field on April 29, 1945, and about 75,000 people attended. Field personnel put together a special nationwide tour in May and June 1945, called "Airborne Attack." Its purpose was to raise funds for the 7th War Bond drive and it visited 51 cities throughout the United States. Mildred Doane, then a 1st Lieutenant in the Army

Entrance to Gate No. 1 of Stout Field circa 1944. USAF

One of the still-existing hangars at Stout Field. Hangars were of permanent construction, built by the WPA under contract before WW II. THOLE

Open House in June 1944 attended by almost 60,000 people. USAF

Photo of a C-47 picking up a CG-4A using the ''snatch'' method. USAF

Another hangar remaining at Stout Field as it was in 1994. THOLE

Nurse Corps, had formerly served 21 months in the Southwest Pacific as a flight nurse before being returned to Stout Field to work in the station hospital. As a member of the tour, she commented on the show: "The airshow was presented in the form of an airborne attack, simulating an actual spearhead, performed by sixty-three officers and enlisted men . . . After the airshow, the planes were on display for the public to have the opportunity of seeing what some of their bonds (were) used for. Also one C-47 Troop Carrier plane was on display all equipped as a hospital plane with litters and all supplies needed in evacuating wounded . . . I demonstrated the procedure of giving blood plasma, how to administer oxygen and many different treatments that are carried out in battle. I also spent much time in answering questions."

Following the end of the war in Europe, Stout Field's operations shifted to an emphasis on the war in the Pacific. Training continued in areas such as gas mask training, small arms familiarization, orientation lectures and films, functional swimming, etc. Flights were still being sent to the ports of debarkation to pick up and transport wounded personnel to hospitals throughout the U.S.

Most formal training stopped on August 16, 1945. In November the Air Force announced that I Troop Carrier Command would be absorbed into IX Troop Carrier Command and its headquarters moved to Greenville Army Air Base, Greenville, South Carolina. This was completed in January 1946. Greenville Army Air Base was formerly used for B-24 and B-25 training and at one time commanded by Col. Oliver Stout. Stout Field was named after Colonel Stout's brother. For several months, Stout Field lay inactive, with just a skeleton crew to maintain the facilities. Only one plane was assigned, used by officers stationed there. There was no transient flying activity. Later, Stout Field came under the control of the 11th Air Force and used as part of the AAF reserve pilot flying proficiency program. Eventually, control of the field reverted to the state. After that, Stout would be used by the Indiana National Guard and the State Police.

Today, Stout Field Army Air Base is still used by the Indiana National Guard as administrative headquarters, and for equipment storage and maintenance. No planes use its runways. The runways are either broken up, used for parking lots, or are foundations for warehouses. Most of the permanent buildings, constructed by the WPA before and early in the war, are still there. They include hangars and the administrative building with the control tower on top. The temporary buildings have long since been removed.

B-17 TRANSITION TRAINING

Hendricks Field

HENDRICKS FIELD was one of the hundreds of Army Air Forces training fields built during the expansion of the Air Force before and during World War II. The decision to build the field was the result of the 30,000 pilot expansion program directed by General Marshall on February 14, 1941. Subsequent expansions would see the Army Air Forces reach a total of 783 main, subbases and auxiliary fields during the Second World War. Originally planned as a basic flying training school, the field's mission was changed to four-engine pilot and crew training while it was nearing the end of construction. Later, the field was used exclusively for B-17 pilot transition. Hendricks Field was located near Sebring, Florida, then a small town in south central Florida. The major sources of income were tourism, citrus growing, cattle ranching, and farming. The population in 1940 was 3,155.

During the summer of 1940, a few civic leaders of Sebring got together and prepared a presentation urging construction of a military base near Sebring. This proposal was taken to Washington by a city councilman, Mr. Higgans, and the city attorney, Mr. Kinsey. Little was heard from the presentation until April 1941, when Major Luke of the Southeast Training Center and John Paul Riddle of Emery-Riddle School of Aviation did an aerial survey of the proposed site. Their findings were positive. After that, the Commanding Officer of the Southeast Training Center, along with others, inspected the site and asked the city for an area totaling approximately 15,000 acres. This was more than the city would negotiate, so a compromise was worked out for 9,200 acres leased for $1 per year. The lease was good for 99 years. Most of the land was palmetto-covered prairie with areas of swamps and brush. The many small ponds and marshy areas caused drainage problems because of the surface water. This affected construction and was a problem after the field was completed. Like many other training fields, Hendricks Field was built far from any major population centers. The nearest large city was Fort Myers, about 60 air miles away.

Construction started during July 1941. The site plan dated September 1941, called for construction of 146 buildings with four runways 150 feet wide and 5,000 feet long. By December 1941, it became clear that construction costs to stabilize the land for a basic training field would be prohibitive. So Col. Carl McDaniel recommended the field be used for combat crew training. This recommendation, along with the recent (December 8, 1941) A-1 priority given to four-engine pilot and crew training, were important considerations in changing the field's mission. As a result, the runways were strengthened and widened to 300 feet. Hendricks Field would be the first B-17 Combat Crew Training school in the United States.

Since the field's location was isolated, roads and a railroad spur were built to the base. This was necessary to get building supplies and workers to the field. One rail unloading point was at a town called DeSoto City that was about two miles from the construction site. From there, material was taken by trucks to the base via an unpaved road. Often, trucks became stuck in the sand and mud during the base's early construction. Considerable clearing was necessary and drainage ditches were dug to help drain some swamp areas and decrease the bug and mosquito problem. Once construction was in full swing, it went on three shifts per day, seven days per week. The number of workers soon exceeded 2,000. Construction workers were desperate for any type housing while working at the base. Single rooms were at a premium, and even those soon vanished with the onslaught of workers and the early military arrivals. Over time, several housing projects were built to help ease the housing shortage. A 193-unit family project was called Highlands Homes and construction began in March 1942 after the base was completed. Another housing project started around the same time. It was built for officers' families, and was nicknamed "Snob Hollow." Many civilian workers lived on the base in housing named "Fortress Place." Some of the first buildings completed were the warehouses for storage of essential material. For a while, Post Headquarters was located in one of the warehouse

Aerial view of Hendricks Field, circa 1946. POLLARD

Aerial view of Hendricks Field taken in 1995. Sebring International Raceway is on the bottom left of the runway complex. THOLE

The former Post Operations building, with the original control tower behind as it appeared in 1995. Today, the Operations Building is the Sebring Flight Center. It contains the airport managers office, pilots lounge and flight services. THOLE

A WW II era hangar in the process of being torn down during early 1995. POLLARD

buildings until an administration building was completed. A cold storage room was available to house perishable items and (because of the heat and high humidity) leather flight jackets, flight suits, and boots. Several of these buildings are still used today. Storage capacity for gasoline totaled 1,000,000 gallons, in ten 25,000-gallon underground tanks and the rest, in above ground tanks.

Hendricks Field was named in January 1942 to honor Lt. Laird W. Hendricks, Jr. Lt. Hendricks was a 1939 graduate of West Point, who began his military service in the Army Coast Artillery and later transferred to the Air Corps. After his transfer to the Army Air Corps, he took pilot training and earned his wings. He was killed in an aircraft accident on July 28, 1941, while in England on a temporary assignment. Lt. Hendricks was born on June 3, 1916, in Ocala, Florida, and was 25 years old when he died. He is buried in Arlington National Cemetery.

The first B-17 was flown into the field by Colonel McDaniel on 29 January 1942. This may have been one of the early model B-17s, probably a B, C, or D (a total of 119 was produced). Some of these early models saw combat; however, others were retained in the States for training purposes. The more advanced models, the E, F, and G (12,597 built) were improved models based upon lessons learned from combat experience. Later, as production of the B-17 caught up with the need, many later models were used for training. Additionally, "war weary" Fortresses were often returned to the States and then used for pilot and crew training. The B-17 G was especially sought after by the pilots being trained for many reasons, one of which was its improved turbo control system.

Combat crew training started in March 1942 with the arrival of 25 crews consisting of pilot, co-pilot and navigators. The class included a Royal Air Force crew and was class SE-42-4-A. By this time, the field had ten B-17s. Crew members involved in the early combat crew training were pilot, co-pilot, navigator, bombardier, engineer, radio operator, and gunners. Crew training never reached a high level of excellence at Hendricks due to shortages of instructors, equipment, proper facilities and time. Additionally, there were problems with the availability, on a timely basis, of crew personnel for training. Often crews left the field before completing their training because of the need for B-17 personnel for combat operations. Late in 1942, following changes in training curriculum, Hendricks Field became a B-17 pilot transition school. On 20 April 1943, the field was

officially designated a B-17 transition field and would serve in this capacity until war's end. By July 1944, there were about 3,700 military personnel and 1,100 civilian personnel on the base, with 81 aircraft of all types. By mid-August 1945, the field had graduated 7,333 B-17 pilots. Early in the field's training program most instructors were selected based upon flying experience and service time. By mid-1944, the situation had changed. Now, recent graduates of advanced flying schools with just over 300 hours flying time were instructing along with the more experienced instructors. The Director of Training then, Col. Calvin Peeler, felt that this was an improvement because of better training techniques and the higher quality of instructors. There was a significant lack of training in formation flying. In 1944, the B-17 Pilot Transition Course was increased to 15 weeks. As a result, more training time was given to current subjects like navigation, and the handling of the aircraft during its bombing run (Bomb Approach). One subject added was Flexible Gunnery. The intent was to give the aircraft commander an appreciation for the role and responsibilities of the plane's gunners. This was a 42-hour course focused on practical work with the fifty caliber machine gun, turrets, and some sighting theory. There was no firing of the machine guns.

Connors Field at Lake Okeechobee, Florida, was assigned to Hendricks as an auxiliary field. This came in handy during times of "blitz training" when the student pilot was required to fly four or five hours daily, seven days a week. Depending upon flying training progress, students flew from five to seven days a week. Two of the more significant reasons for the canceling of flying activity were high winds caused by thunder storms and hurricanes, and the smoke from an occasional swamp fire. Fires were sometimes started by exhaust particles from the B-17 engines.

A significant training milestone was reached on 25 November 1945 when the 500,000th landing was made by an aircraft flown by 2nd Lt. Robert Osterbert. His training plane number was 31 and he touched down at 9:52 PM. B-17s flown by student pilots were involved in eight fatal crashes while in training at Hendricks Field, a total of 44 men were killed. The first accident happened on April 15, 1942, when a B-17 was lost on a round-trip navigation flight to Brownsville, Texas. The plane was suspected to have crashed into the Gulf of Mexico. The last fatal accident occurred on July 14, 1945, when a B-17 went down about three miles from the base.

Jim Green, a new pilot, just graduated from advanced flying school with 210 flying hours when he arrived at Hendricks in March 1944 for transition training. He recalls the upper and lower classes, and marching in formation to all activities, including meals, physical training, and the flight line. Only field grade officers were excused from marching. This didn't sit well with some students, one of which was a Captain with over 1,000 flying hours. The crews were typically two pilots and an engineer. The instructor would fly with the two pilots only as needed for training purposes and to check progress. He would then be the fourth member of the crew. Jim was never impressed with the B-17's speed, because most training missions were flown at 150 mph. On one of his flights, he decided to see just how fast the plane would go. So, he rolled in some trim tab, pushed on the yoke and dived the ship. The best he could do was around 280 mph. No one would ever convince him the B-17 could go faster. He remembers formation flying as the toughest part of his training. Often, when returning from a single plane training flight, he joined a returning formation to gain a higher landing priority because formations were normally landed first. Jim remembers most graduates being sent to Tampa, Florida, for reassignment. There they were joined with a crew and went to either MacDill Field, Drew Field, or Avon Park Army Air Field for crew training.

Hendricks Field assumed an additional training responsibility in May 1945, when the base was ordered to train (on an urgent basis) 25 emergency rescue crews. Apparently, the Emergency Rescue School at Keesler Field, Mississippi, did not have the capacity to train needed additional crews. The training required special B-17s that were sent to Hendricks. Crew members for the emergency rescue planes were pilot, co-pilot, navigator, engineer, radio operator-gunner, two waist searchers, one tail searcher, and a radar observer. The training at Hendricks required about four days. It included procedures to drop the emergency boat (Higgins Boats) from an especially equipped B-17, navigation training, and emergency rescue training. Kessler Field furnished many instructors.

A good look at B-17 transition training in 1945 is given by Bob Schultz, who was assigned to Hendricks Field in May 1945. To Bob the B-17 was huge in comparison to the other planes he had been flying, one of which was the P-40. Over time, he grew to love the B-17. Bob's training started in June. At this time, the transition course lasted ten weeks and pilots were required to accumulate 105 hours flying the plane. Everyone in Bob's class was an officer, including some who were lieutenant colonels.

Training missions were usually four to five hours long with the student switching off to another student pilot after about a half hour's flying time. The B-17 was a large aircraft for its time and without power boosts for the controls flying could become very fatiguing. This was especially true during formation practice when the pilot was required to keep the wings within ten feet of the other aircraft. During formation flying, pilots usually rotated handling the controls every fifteen minutes. This type of flying was not only fatiguing but also hazardous. This was especially true with pilots, new to the B-17, flying in close proximity while fighting the prop wash of the nearby aircraft. Formation practice included changing formations on command while in the air. Simple maneuvers were tried first, then the students moved on to the more complex flying required by difficult formations, like the "Box" and "Stepped Down V." Bob recalls another group losing a B-17, during formation practice, when it crashed following a collision with another Fortress while in a formation change.

Bob believes his toughest flying was learning emergency engine out procedures, especially when the instructor would cut both engines on the same side of the aircraft. With two engines out it required all his 140 lbs. and both feet on the rudder pedal to maintain direction. The instructors were also fond of pulling two engines on takeoff after the plane had gained some altitude and the wheels had retracted. His responsibility then was to maintain altitude and direction, trim the plane, feather the windmilling props, and get the plane lined up for landing.

He also learned procedures to transfer fuel among the many different tanks to maintain the proper trim and balance, night and instrument flying, and simulated bombing missions. While the B-17 was a relatively stable aircraft it still took some getting used to because the pilot's seat was about 20 feet off the ground. This was a challenging transition for a pilot just recently transferred from flying P-40s. Student pilots often abused the plane, especially while learning proper landing technique. If the landing was too rough it occasionally caused the gear to break off and rip through the cabin and tail of the plane. The solution was to concentrate on a three-point or slightly tail-first landing.

This flight training was reinforced by ground school where he learned the aircraft's systems, weather, instrument flying in the Link trainer, some

Rear view of former control tower. THOLE

Former warehouses, still in use. One has been refurbished. SCHOTT

The Hendricks Field machine shop located near the sub-depot hangar. After the war, an engine overhaul company used this building. SCHOTT

One of the original hangars still remaining. It may have been the sub-depot hangar. SCHOTT

Original Hendricks Field fire station, still in use today, as a fire station. THOLE

The entrance to Hendricks Field, as it was in 1995, with part of the Sebring International Raceway to the right of the entrance sign. THOLE

Another aerial view of the field with the former warehouse area in the foreground and the water tower and ramp area in the background. THOLE

Walt Pierce standing in front of his beautifully restored Stearman "Ol Smokey."
THOLE

Interior view of former WW II hangar in the process of being torn down, 1995. Note extensive use of wood beams reflecting the shortage of steel during the war. This "temporary" building still stands after years of use. THOLE

training with the secret Norden bomb sight, and much more. At this point in the war, pilots were also required to learn the responsibilities of other members of their crew, including the radio operator, the navigator, the engineer, and gunners.

Sebring, Florida, was hot and humid especially while Bob was at Hendricks. "Early morning flights were absolute misery until we took off," he recalls. "The daily rain showers bred mosquitoes, and they would congregate at night inside the cockpits. Sitting in a cockpit with no breeze, trying to follow a complicated checklist, the pilot would nearly go crazy from the bugs until he could get the plane rolling and off the ground. On afternoon flights, the problem was heat that made metal surfaces on the aircraft almost too hot to touch." Bob was one of the first two pilots in his class to solo both day and night. He graduated as a First Pilot on July 28, 1945.

The first B-29 to land at Hendricks Field arrived on January 27, 1945. It was flown by Major Titensor, a former instructor at the field, who was stationed at Harvard Army Air Field, Harvard, Nebraska. A special guard detail was assigned to maintain the security of the plane. By this time, pilots and other crew members were being selected for B-29 training and assignment to the B-29 training bases. By April, policies were established to outline requirements for B-29 upgrade training. The Station Diary for June reported that the Eastern Flying Training Command would soon require the names of 60 B-17 pilots with 1,500 or more hours for training in B-29s.

Activity at Hendricks Field slowed after the end of the war with Japan. In September 1945, fourteen B-17s were flown to Walnut Ridge Army Air Field, Walnut Ridge, Arkansas, for storage. Transition training of pilots, co-pilots and flight engineers was scheduled to stop in mid-August 1945. However, some training may have continued through October. By then, orders were received for all students to be put into continuation training, except Classes 725, 825, and West Point graduates. Other flight training continued, as did some ground school and Link training. By early December, instructions were received to transfer all single engine pilots to Moody Field, Valdosta, Georgia. The twin-engine pilots along with

150 four-engine pilots were to be transferred to Columbus Army Air Field, Columbus, Mississippi. On 8 December all four-engine training stopped and on 11 December the B-17s were grounded, pending transfer. On 15 December, the B-17s were flown to Smyrna Army Air Base, Smyrna, Tennessee. Hendricks Field was scheduled to be closed down on December 31, 1945.

By late 1945, most of the civilian personnel had left, only three remained in the Training and Operations department. Colonel Farr left the field on January 1, 1946; however, a small contingent of Army Air Force personnel were still on the field as late as mid-1946, disposing of surplus equipment. Some equipment was transferred to other bases and salvage and surplus sales were held on the base. The Federal Public Housing Authority released 54 two-story wooden barracks to the University of Florida for conversion to family apartment units. Initially the City of Sebring turned down the offer of the field from the government because of the financial liability the city would face maintaining the field. Eventually, it was declared Surplus Property and later the city took over the field. The field was then renamed "Sebring Air Terminal." However, facilities deteriorated as attempts were made by the civic leaders and business people of Sebring to turn the field into a profitable operation. Many structures were demolished, some were sold and moved to other locations.

Hendricks Field's first Commanding Officer was, Col. Leonard H. Rodieck, who helped design and supervise the field's construction while project officer. Col. Carl B. McDaniel was the Field's second commander and assumed command on 6 December 1941. Col. Warren H. Higgins was the third commander from 26 October 1943 to 15 June 1945, the fourth and last commander was Col. Charles D. Farr, who held the distinction of earning both the Navy and the Air Force Wings.

Today, the field is a growing industrial park and the site of the annual Sebring Auto Race. A few buildings remain as reminders of the former air base's proud service during WW II. The field's name today is Sebring Regional Airport.

B-24 TRANSITION TRAINING

Smyrna Army Air Field

SMYRNA ARMY AIR FIELD was the first of the B-24 pilot transition schools, graduating its original class of 44 officer and civilian pilots on August 14, 1942. The airfield was named after the nearby town of Smyrna, Tennessee. Smyrna is about twenty miles southeast from the center of Nashville, and twelve miles northwest of Murfreesboro. Its population in 1940 was about 500 people, and today, the population is near 14,000. The field itself is located 3.5 miles from Interstate 24 off exit 66, about two miles from Smyrna. The former training field, now called Smyrna Airport, is the third largest airfield in the State of Tennessee.

The decision to build a base at Smyrna was made by the War Department on December 10, 1941. This decision was made after site selection surveys, which included a review of the facilities available in the nearby communities, meetings with state and local officials (including the Nashville Chamber of Commerce) and the Corps of Engineers of the Nashville District. Other cities being considered at the time were De Ridder, Louisiana; Jackson, Mississippi; and Greenville, South Carolina. Eventually, each of these cities would have an Army Air Base. As early as September, the site had been approved as suitable, and recommended that it be obtained "as a station for a heavy bombardment group." The land was acquired by lease from the State for $1.00 per year, renewable for 25 years. It was one of the 14 bases that the War Department had planned for training of heavy bombardment groups during the latter part of 1941. The land for the base was available because of the Tennessee State Legislature's House Bill No. 669, which authorized raising $1,000,000 "for the purpose of providing funds to acquire lands in the name of the State for the purpose of State and National Defense, and providing for the lease of said lands by the Governor—to be used as part of the National Defense Program." The Act passed on February 11, 1941. In the event the land could not be purchased, leased, or gotten by negotiation, the act provided for taking the land by condemnation under the laws of eminent domain.

As mentioned, the four-man site selection board led by Col. Jacob Wuest, finished its review of the nearly 3,300 acres of offered land on September 10, 1941, and recommended it very favorably. After the site selection board made its recommendation, a group of citizens lead by Governor Prentice Cooper, along with the Mayor of Nashville and the Manager of the Nashville Chamber of Commerce, made a trip to Washington to make their case for the base. The group met with General Arnold and others and received a favorable reaction. Washington approved the site on December 10, 1941. On January 1, 1942, Governor Cooper announced Washington's decision to build at Smyrna, and stated "the intention of the state and the cities associated with it to acquire this land at once and the intention of the federal government to occupy it within about 30 days."

Local reaction to the new military facility was generally positive, except for the people living on the base site. At the time, the land was prime farm land with almost 3,000 acres under cultivation. The area contained about thirty homes, with 35 separate parcels of land, some of which had been in the same family for almost a 100 years. *The Rutherford Courier*, in its December 19, 1941 edition, reported, "Many are disposing of their household furnishings and livestock at auction sales. Indications are that a great many of the families will move into Smyrna, Murfreesboro, and Nashville or to other farm lands in Middle Tennessee." The paper also reported that $300,000 would be needed for purchasing the land. Later, more money was needed. Most land was bought by the State; however, some owners would not sell, and their property was taken by condemnation. In general, the price paid for the land was about $140 per acre.

Originally, the field was to be used for the training of heavy bombardment groups; however, it was never used for this purpose. Plans had been made and sites selected to establish four bombing ranges as part of the school, but this never happened. When activated, the school was called the Army Air Forces Combat Crew School, but this was a misnomer

Aerial view of Smyrna Army Air Field, 1942. By this time, the initial construction had been completed and training was in progress. New construction was in progress, note the third runway being built. USAF

because full crews were not trained here. Instead, the field was used to train pilots to fly the B-24. This assignment was the result of the decision to take over the training then being handled by the Transcontinental and Western Air School at Albuquerque, New Mexico. At the time, Transcontinental was giving transition training to ferrying crews for the Ferrying Division of the Air Transport command. Smyrna Army Air Field also did some transition training in the B-17 as well, but this lasted only a few months, from November 1942 to March 1943. This training was transferred to the newly opened B-17 pilot school at Lockbourne Army Air Base in Columbus, Ohio. The transition training of ferrying crews along with pilot training continued until January 1943 when the training of ferrying crews was stopped. Then the school was renamed the Army Air Forces Pilot Transition School (Four Engine). From then until the end of the war, the school received pilots who had graduated from advanced flying school, and trained them to fly the B-24. From

there, most graduates were sent to the Operational Training Units and later to combat. Others were retained as instructors, and some went to the School of Applied Tactics at Orlando, Florida.

The initial design work for the new airbase started on December 16, 1942, by the District Engineer's office in Nashville. This work focused on grading, draining, and paving projects. On January 2, 1942, construction was authorized, and actual construction started on the twelfth. However, poor weather in February, March, and the first part of April slowed work considerably. By early July, most of the basic airfield was completed. This included the troop housing and two runways (each 300 feet wide and 5,500 feet long) which still required some grading. The hangars were not finished. Delaying the finish of the squadron hangars was the lack of steel rollers for the hangar doors. The first phase of construction was ending by June, with about 175 buildings of the "mobilization" type completed or near completion. "Mobilization" buildings were considered semi-permanent construction and were made from wood and heated by coal. The mobilization building was better looking than the "theater of operations" type building and in the case of the barracks was two story as opposed to one story for the "theater of operations" buildings. The construction process was speeded considerably by precut and measured wood and the use of pipes, that arrived cut and threaded. The field was activated on June 1, 1942, with then Lt. Col. Troop Miller in command. This was a temporary measure until June 3, when Colonel Stanley Umstead arrived from temporary assignment to take command of the field. At the time, Colonel Umstead had been arranging for the militarization of the Jack Frye Four Engine School, and the transfer of the school from Albuquerque, New Mexico, to Smyrna. Colonel Umstead remained in command until March 22, 1945, when he was replaced by Colonel Richard H. Ballard, who stayed until October 1945. Before taking command of Smyrna Army Air Field, Colonel Umstead was well known for his test pilot work with the Douglas XB-19, a huge four-engine bomber. At the time, it was the largest American aircraft ever built. Colonel Umstead's daughter, Patricia, was married on the post in Chapel No.1 in August 1944, to First Lieutenant Richard Eaton. The reception was held in the Officer's Club.

Considerable work was needed to complete the field. A progress report dated June 17 said, "troop housing is 100% complete, operating buildings 96%, and ordnance area 10%. All equipment for completion of electric power system has been shipped from manufacturers. Control tower will be completed by 10 July 1942. Construction of the water system is progressing very satisfactory." Construction was in progress everywhere, drinking water was transported to the base in tank trucks from the town of Smyrna, and military personnel and the civilian workers ate at a construction company facility outside the gate. Camp Forest, an Army training post located about fifty miles southeast, at Tullahoma, supplied bedding for the first group of men at Smyrna, and food during June. The hospital was not opened until July. Before that time, Camp Forest was used along with the Veterans' Hospital at Murfreesboro. Cars and trucks were borrowed from Camp Forest, Perry Field in Nashville, and from the Area Engineer. The transportation situation eased with the arrival of 97 men and 26 vehicles from Bolling Field, Washington, D.C. to form the 313th Air Base Squadron. To help maintain the aircraft the 571st School Squadron came to

the field in June and on July 1, the 572nd came from Kirkland Field, Albuquerque, New Mexico, and brought with them additional men and equipment. Also in June, the 660th, and then in July, the 665th School Squadrons filled out with personnel at Hendricks Field in Sebring, Florida, arrived at Smyrna. From this small number of Army Air Forces personnel the base would rapidly grow to 2,419 enlisted men by October 1942. In June 1945, the post had 2,677 enlisted men permanently assigned along with 639 officers. Civilian employees hired to work at the Sub-Depot were recruited at Berry Field (Nashville) by the 100th Sub-Depot following its start up in mid-May. By the end of October 1944, there were at least 1,209 civilian employees working at Smyrna. Smyrna's field headquarters was in a training building which also housed other departments such as the hospital staff and operations. Shortages of personnel and equipment were common. This was typical at most of the new training bases as they prepared to begin their training function. It could not have been a pleasant sight for the newly arriving cadets and the training personnel. However, training was about to start and everyone prepared to begin with what was available.

The school was officially opened on July 4, 1942. At the time, there were 215 buildings of all types on the base including 51 enlisted men's barracks and 10 Bachelor Officer's quarters. An "Open House" was held the day the field officially opened, and visitors from the adjoining communities were invited to the field to view this newest addition to the Army Air Force's growing chain of training fields. Guests included the Governor of Tennessee, Prentice Cooper, along with the Mayors of Nashville, Murfreesboro, and Smyrna. The guests toured the facilities including the barracks, mess halls, chapel, the Link training facility, and saw the B-24, up close. General Arnold, Chief of the Army Air Forces, toured the base on July 9.

Though the school was opened on July 4, much needed to be done before training could start. The first need was for planes and pilots with experience to instruct in their use. Smyrna received its first B-24 around July 1 when it was flown in from Albuquerque, New Mexico, by Lieutenant Maxwell, a former RCAF pilot. The same day, sixteen men able to fly B-24s were loaded aboard the same plane and flew back to Albuquerque. The next day they returned flying an additional seven B-24s to Smyrna. It is not clear if the planes came from Kirkland Field or Albuquerque Army Air Field. Both airfields were located

Another 1942 view of Smyrna showing the center part of the base with the headquarters buildings. In the far background is the water tower with the hangars to the left and right on the flight line. The water tower is still on the field today. USAF

This 1942 picture shows the housing area, probably student officers quarters, in the picture's foreground. USAF

Officers in class learning Morse Code. The class is being taught by a WAC during 1943. USAF

Ground school class on radio being given to student pilots in 1943. USAF

WW II barracks refurbished over the years, this is how they looked in 1994. THOLE

Today's view of a former WW II hangar. THOLE

Another picture of a former WW II barracks that has been refurbished. THOLE

This is building #621, the Consolidated Maintenance hangar as it was in 1994. THOLE

This may be the remains of a Group headquarters building. Today it is derelict and used for storage. THOLE

in Albuquerque. By July 18, there were 32 B-24s at Smyrna mostly, B-24Ds and one B-24A. The most planes available at the field at any one time in 1942 were 34 in November. Before flying training could begin, the instructors were required to train themselves on flying the B-24 because many had very little solo time on the aircraft. In June 1942, there were no specific plans or programs coming from other headquarters on just how to run a B-24 pilot transition school. Smyrna was basically on its own and would be for some time. Broad goals and objectives were given by Training Command, but, how to get it done was pretty much up to the personnel on the line at Smyrna. Smyrna was the first, and would pave the way for the others to follow. We were in a war on a scale never before experienced. So everything

was scarce, especially the trained personnel and time necessary to carry out the largest flying training program the world had ever seen. So programs were designed, and what worked was kept, and what did not, was replaced. The first class, 42-4-J, started on July 16th, and by the end of 1942, 561 pilots graduated. There were no fatalities. The first class was made up of both civilian and military personnel from the Ferry Command. Most of the officers had been directly commissioned into the service and had little knowledge or appreciation for the Army way of doing things. This class graduated with 28 hours of transition flying and 34 hours of ground school. The field's official history reported: "The civilians had been old barnstorming pilots, and flying circus, stunt, and commercial pilots. They were

The Officers Club Pavilion as it appeared in 1943. The band stand is in the upper right of picture. USAF

Remains of what may have been the Officers Club Pavilion as shown in top photo. Note the former band stand in upper right of picture. THOLE

not dependable." This comment was probably made because of the civilians' reluctance to conform to the rigid structure of life on an Army post, far removed from the major population centers. The civilian flyers had come from many different backgrounds and were used to acting independently. Many had been their own bosses and found doing things the Army way stifling. Most were excellent flyers who were now forced to learn to fly "by the numbers." Later, in 1942, Smyrna received a total of 27 former Transcontinental and Western Airline pilots for training in the B-24. It was decided that these flyers did not have the background to qualify as four-engine pilots and most lacked night flying and instrument experience. It was also felt that the Transcontinental and Western pilots were "not quality pilots." However, the majority probably graduated.

Former American Airlines pilots also received training during 1942 at Smyrna.

Ernest Gann the well-known author of *The High And The Mighty, Fate Is The Hunter* and many other books took some training at Smyrna. He reports it as being "perfunctory," about six hours worth in a B-24. This "training" was given during the time he was engaged in flying cargo for the Air Transport Command. Later, Mr. Gann would fly the C-87 (cargo version of the B-24). He had this to say about the plane: "They were an evil bastard contraption, nothing like the relatively efficient B-24 except in appearance. In time they betrayed each of us in various ways and there was a tendency to approach one as if it were an angry bull elephant—to which they somehow bore a startling resemblance."

Keeping the B-24s flying was the responsibility

of the 100th Sub-Depot personnel and mechanics assigned to the training squadrons. Major repairs were done at the Sub-Depot while minor maintenance was handled by the squadron mechanics. The start-up staff for the Sub-Depot came from the Second Sub-depot at Turner Field in Albany, Georgia. Early members of the Sub-Depot were inexperienced and spent much of their time reading appropriate material about the B-24 and learning about the plane via on-the-job training. Besides maintaining their planes, the Sub-Depot had the additional responsibility to order all supplies and equipment necessary to keep the planes flying. At the start up, the Sub-Depot had three civilian employees, and by the end of January 1944, there were 399 civilians working at the Sub-Depot.

Inexperienced maintenance people, rough usage by student pilots, and the lack of experience working with a relatively new bomber design, combined to cause significant operational problems with the big bomber. Some major concerns were gas tank leaks (a common problem with the B-24), nose and main gear shimmy, generator failures, propeller governor failures and difficulty with the cowl flap motors. One particularly worrisome problem was excessive flexibility and failure of some horizontal stabilizers. Eventually, this caused 15 aircraft to be grounded. Some B-24s were sent to San Antonio, Texas, for modifications to the horizontal stabilizer. As a result, two classes graduated without the required number of flying hours.

The responsibility for the training of the B-24 pilots at Smyrna was carried by Col. Troop Miller Jr. as the Director of Training. Colonel Miller set the training program and organized the ground school along with his other responsibilities. This included planning and supervising building construction. There were no specific training directives from a higher headquarters because at the time, there was not much experience in the mass training of B-24 pilots. What little there was, would come from the newly opened B-17 pilot transition school at Sebring, Florida (Hendricks Field) and the now transferred B-24 school at Albuquerque, New Mexico.

The experience gained with the first two classes was a factor in increasing the flying training time from 28 hours to 50. It was also recommended that ground school be increased from 34 hours to 100 hours for pilots and co-pilots. The additional flying hours instruction started with class "L." This was the third class at Smyrna and began training during August 1942. The fifty hours flying time were broken

down as follows, 20 for transition flying, 20 for navigation (12 during the day and eight at night), eight hours on instruments, and two hours solo. The schedule was flexible and could be adjusted for those needing more transition experience.

Starting with the fourth-class (162 students) the classes were broken into groups and then into training squadrons. Not all groups received the same training, because the training was based upon need and experience of the students. The third class (Class "L") was the first to receive instruction in night flying. The first two classes received none, because the field had no night lighting equipment. Some ground school subjects at the time included operation of the Hydromatic Propellers, fuel, oil, and electrical systems, first aid (two hours), chemical warfare, and practical navigation (12 hours). At this time, Ferrying Command crews were made up of pilot, co-pilot, flight engineer, and radio operator. Also, other students were sent to Smyrna for instruction from the Golf Coast Training Center. During the early part of Smyrna's training, the classes contained a mixture of civilian, and military pilots. Some had considerable flying experience, while others were newly minted Second Lieutenants with 200 hours total time on single and twin engine planes.

During the later part of 1942 and into early 1943, some training with the B-17 took place at Smyrna. The aircraft were newly manufactured and flown into the base. Since there were no instructors qualified to teach the B-17, they came from the B-17 school at Sebring, Florida. By this time, there were eight training squadrons at Smyrna (the 571st, 572nd, 660th, 665th, 1037th, 1038th, 1039th, and the 313th). The reason for the temporary training on the B-17 was the availability of the B-17, and the shortage in the production of the B-24. By March 1943, the situation had corrected itself. The students and the B-17s were sent to Lockbourne Army Air Base near Columbus, Ohio. This ended B-17 training at Smyrna. By mid-1943 there were approximately 60 B-24s at Smyrna and in September the Central Instructors School was started. This meant the base was selected to train B-24 instructors besides its primary role of training B-24 pilots. At this time, Smyrna was the only B-24 instructor school in the country. During 1943, the school graduated 1,640 pilots (including four from Yugoslavia) from a total of 14 classes. This included students from the nine-week transition course, the Central Instructors Course, and the four-and-a-half week Instructor Trainee course. A total of 156 students had failed to graduate the school.

. . .

Smyrna B-24s in formation. USAF

· · ·

Interior view of PX no. 2, cafeteria. When the base first opened, the PX was housed in a no frills military building that had plain wooden shelves, no display cases, poor lighting, and inadequate ventilation. As time and resources allowed, the PXs were upgraded. They offered refreshments; i.e., cola, beer, hamburgers, etc., and a variety of merchandise for sale to the soldiers and their families.

Guard Mount, 1039th Guard Squadron, with B-24 and a hangar in the background, 1943. USAF

. . .

Interior view of Chapel no. 2, 1943. USAF

Interior view of the Link trainer building. The Link trainers are on the left and the instructors desks are to the right, 1943. USAF

In August 1943, Smyrna became home to the 76th Flying Training Wing. The purpose of this organization was to monitor and coordinate the training of several other training fields. They were the B-17 school at Lockbourne Army Air Base at Columbus, Ohio, the B-17 schools at Hendricks Field in Sebring, Florida, the B-17 school at Chanute Field in Rantoul, Illinois, and the B-24 school at Maxwell Field in Montgomery, Alabama.

Normally, the Commanding Officer of the field, Colonel Umstead, would write a progress report to the Commanding General of the Southeast Training Command giving his views on each class following their graduation. His comments reflected the need to move the B-24 pilots along and that training was not always as thorough as everyone would have liked. Here are some of his comments about

class 42-4-0, the first to graduate in 1943. "The general average flying ability of this class was found to be below that of the last class 42-4-M, with but very few exceptions . . . Inability to fly instruments properly, and particularly to think of courses, altitudes and speeds at the same time, was the main difficulty encountered by the majority of the class and was the major weakness of the class as a whole. Only 23 students were able to qualify for issuance of Instrument Cards. The remainder of the class will require more supervised practice and experience to safely handle a B-24 airplane under instrument conditions." Of Class 43-4-A, the second to graduate in 1943, he had this to say . . . "This class was below the standard of previous classes but with twenty additional hours of instruction added, the standard of profi- was attained. Again lack of basic knowledge

A Squadron Day Room, circa 1943. USAF

An overview of several WW II buildings remaining at Smyrna as they were in 1994. THOLE

of instrument flying was the chief weakness, thirty-eight students finally being issued Instrument Ratings. The phase of weakness of the remainder was forwarded to their new stations and it is believed all will be capable instrument pilots with a minimum of additional practice on their phases . . ." He had this to say about Class 43-4-X (graduated August 5, 1943): "The attitude of the students in this class as a whole was very poor. The students showed little regard for punctuality or for military customs and courtesy. One student made an unauthorized cross-country and engaged in low flying while on this cross-country, in violation of CAA and Air Force regulations . . ." This was a special class at Smyrna made up of former B-25 and B-26 pilots with very little instrument time. Apparently these students were sent to Smyrna to fill a quota for B-24 pilots and some may not have been too happy about being transferred from the comparatively fast and maneuverable B-25s and B-26s to the lumbering B-24.

By January 1943, most students were now graduates of twin-engine advanced schools and had rather limited flying experience. The modifications made in time and course content since the school opened in 1942 were the result of lessons learned and the dictates of combat. Flying training included instruments, formation altitude missions, navigation, and practice in the Link trainer. Ground school courses included maintenance, navigation, radio, meteorology, and the use of oxygen. Additional changes and additions were made in late 1943. By March, ground school for Transition Pilots was increased to 152 hours and by January 1944 was 171 hours of lecture. When the school opened in 1942 there were few if any training aids available. Over time, as equipment became available training aids were constructed, some of it made from planes damaged in training accidents or no longer fit to fly. Training aids available in 1943 included a Pratt & Whitney engine, Hamilton Standard propeller, a top turret, brake system, life raft, the fuel transfer system, and complete radio system. The Flying Training Command was becoming more involved in training course content and time required to complete each phase. Attempts were made to standardize by taking advantage of the lessons learned from combat and the experience gained from student training. These ideas were passed to the various training schools. As a result, the quality of training in late 1943 was much improved. Colonel Troop Miller Jr., who had been in charge of Smyrna's training since the base opened, was transferred to a new four-engine school at Maxwell Field in mid-1943. He was replaced by Colonel Cain who was instrumental in the standardization of the organization and flying training curriculum. Three fields were added as auxiliary fields. They were Campbell Army Air Field, Camp Campbell, Tennessee, William Northern Field, Tullahoma, Tennessee, and Berry Field, Nashville, Tennessee.

Flying Training Command tried to duplicate the problems in training that would be faced by the new pilots in combat. One problem was teaching the student to take off with the weight of the aircraft as it would be loaded for a bombing mission. Since it was not practical to load each aircraft with bombs, ammunition, machine guns, full crews etc., the decision was made to make the training takeoffs using less than maximum power. This was somewhat difficult to do because the training fields were limited to 91 octane fuel versus the 100 octane used by the crews in combat. When Smyrna began using the reduced octane fuel, 1,741 pounds of armament were removed from each plane.

By 1944, time spent by the student pilot in the transition course had been extended to 105 flying hours over a 10-week transition course. The course was broken out as follows, transition to the B-24, instrument flying, navigation, practice with formation flying, flying at high altitudes, and bomb approach training. Bomb approach training was added in August 1943. This part of the new pilot's instruction was intended to help him better work with the bombardier while approaching the target to improve the accuracy of the bomb drop. The course included actual flying and considerable work with the Norden bomb sight under simulated bomb run conditions. Some of it was done in a classroom setting. Aerial gunnery was added in October 1944. This was intended to help the pilot better appreciate the role of the gunners on his ship, how the systems worked, and what the pilot could do to improve the results of his gunners. The pilots studied the 50 cal. machine gun and the turrets; however, they did no live firing of the weapons at Smyrna. For a short period in 1944, there were more transition pilots than the school could handle, so the transition period was extended to 15 weeks. The extra five weeks were considered "pre-transition" and spent in ground school, where the B-24 pilot-to-be spent most of his time working and learning about the mechanical functions of his aircraft at the maintenance hangars and the classroom. By late 1944, the glut of transition pilots had passed and the school returned to ten weeks.

By January 1945, there were 101 B-24s at Smyrna being used for training and were averaging 17,000 to 18,000 landings per month. The school had trained a total of 6,406 pilots to fly the B-24 (with some learning on the B-17) from its first class in 1942 to the last graduation in October 1945. These numbers may actually be higher because of some confusion in the list of graduating classes. The greatest number, 2,774, graduated in 1944. Flying training continued until August 14, 1945, when for a brief period, it was stopped. Some training resumed but on a much reduced basis. About 80 B-24s went to Walnut Ridge Army Air Field, Arkansas, for storage, and 25 were kept at the field to complete the training of Class 825, which was made up of graduates from West Point. There was no further transition training at Smyrna after October 31, 1945. At this point, the fate of the field was uncertain and very little was being done except to maintain the facilities, inventory and store equipment, and complete paper work. Some departments had completely shut down due to lack of personnel. By the end of November, all remaining B-24s had been transferred from Smyrna, and the sound of the big Pratt & Whitneys would not be heard again. During this period, some pilots assigned to Smyrna, were transferring about 450 B-24s from Greenville, Mississippi, to Walnut Ridge for storage. Late in November, flying began with 22 B-17s flown in from Lubbock and Fort Worth Army Air Fields in Texas. In December another 31

B-17s arrived from Hendricks Field, in Sebring, Florida, along with some pilots and support personnel. During November, December, and January 1946, there was no new pilot training at the field. The flying that was done was to maintain proficiency and learn to fly the B-17s by pilots assigned to Smyrna. Additionally, some pilots were involved in flying surplus aircraft to various storage sites.

In June 1947 Smyrna Army Air Field was put on the inactive list. Little happened except to maintain the facilities until the government decided what to do with the facility. The base was reopened in September 1948 as Smyrna Air Force Base. Later in 1950, it was renamed Sewart Air Force Base to honor Major Allan J. Sewart, a native of Nashville, Tennessee, who was killed during a bombing mission in World War II. The base was home to C-119s, C-123s, C-130s and for a while in 1955 was the Air Force's helicopter training center flying H-21s. The base was closed again in 1970. Today it is the Smyrna Airport owned by the Smyrna Rutherford County Airport Authority. Considerable time and effort have been spent to improve the field, which is the third largest in the state. It still maintains a military presence with units of the National Guard. Many buildings and facilities remain from the World War II period and are in excellent condition, which can be attributed to the almost constant presence of the military through 1970. Most of the buildings have been updated and are still in use.

Aerial view of the former air base circa, 1990. Note the size of the hangars and the large building directly behind them. This was White Hall, built to house 2,200 troops and at one time, the largest military structure in the United States. BOUDREAUX

TECHNICAL TRAINING

Chanute Air Force Base

CHANUTE AIR FORCE BASE was built in 1917 because the War Department decided to improve the strength of the Aviation Section of the Army's Signal Corps. As part of this build up, ground schools were opened at six colleges. Also, twenty-seven flying schools were established to train new pilots. A site near the small Village of Rantoul, Illinois (1917 population — 1,400) was selected for a new training field. The contract to build was let on May 22, 1917. The base is named to honor Octave Chanute (1832–1910), a world renowned engineer, aviation historian, and pioneer of heavier-than-air flight. He was also a consultant for the Wright brothers. The building area consisted of 640 acres (the base would later grow to over 2,000 acres) and was leased to the government. The area was level, serviced by a railroad, and had a source of water and electricity from the Village of Rantoul. Poor weather delayed serious construction until early June 1917. The government had given the contractor (English Brothers Construction Company) sixty days to complete the field, so construction went on at a breakneck pace. Soon, over 1,500 men were at work seven days a week clearing the fields and putting up the wood frame buildings. The building phase of Chanute Field was almost completed by the late July deadline. The cost was about $1 million. By mid-August, the contractors had left, and the then-Commander, Major Dunsworth closed the field to unauthorized personnel. At this time, the field had about fifty major buildings, twelve of which were hangars.

Flying training had already begun on July 18, while the field was still under construction. The first airplane, a biplane flown by Captain William W. Spain, arrived on July 4. Later in the month, on July 9, 23 Curtiss Jennies of the 16th Aero Squadron flew in from Ashburn Field near Chicago. They were the first planes used for training. In the evening of the same day, a train with 25 carloads of men and equipment arrived to complete the initial build up. Later in 1918, the flying training was increased to 120 hours. After the course was successfully completed, the student was required to pass many flying tests to become a Reserve Military Aviator. After that, the student went to Chicago to take a physical exam. If successful, he would be commissioned a First Lieutenant and assigned to duty with a military unit. The decision was made in late 1917 to stop flying training because of deteriorating weather conditions. However, the field remained opened and the em-

phasis shifted to technical training.

Some minor improvements were made at the post at this time to make it more comfortable in the winter. Some lighting was added and parts of the grass flying field were given a gravel surface similar to a gravel road. After the severe winter of 1917/1918, the field prepared to start flying training in the spring. During this period, additional improvements were made, and by March there were about 1,500 men stationed at Chanute. The number of men stationed at the field would vary considerably depending upon its mission at the time. Flying training began on the 10th of April and an auxiliary field of 103 acres was added to give the flying students additional room to practice landings. The training tempo increased and by late May, the men were getting up at 4:45 AM and working until sunset. This schedule was later eased. Formation flying was added to the curriculum, as was night flying. A machine gun and rifle range were built on the southeast corner of the field and nicknamed "The Eastern Front." Technical training continued, and by now, Chanute had a photo section that taught aerial photography procedures.

With the end of the war, Chanute again stopped flying training. The field's contribution to the war effort was considerable. It was one of the smallest training fields, yet it trained about 525 pilots (twice as many as the average training field), and played host to 18 Aero Squadrons. However, by November 1919, there were only a few officers and enlisted men left on the field. During this time, Chanute was a storage depot for OX-5 aircraft engines and paint. The field continued to deteriorate until 1921 when it gained a new lease on life. Early in January 1921, The Air Service Mechanics School was transferred from Kelley Field to Chanute, and would prove to be a major new mission for Chanute. Over 800 men and 90 rail cars of equipment were transferred to the field.

Along with the mechanics school, Chanute also picked up the Air Service Photographic School, formerly based at Langley Field, Virginia. Another training department was added later in 1921, with the addition of the Air Service Communications School from Ft. Sill, Oklahoma. After the three schools merged, the name was changed in 1926 to the Air Corps Technical School. Some additional improvements were made at the field, including the construction of nine steel hangars. This would be the last significant improvement until 1938. Mean-

(0.91.-8630-CFPS)(16-10-10A)(12':1500')(CHANUTE FIELD CONST.)

Aerial view of Chanute Air Force Base in 1940 during its massive expansion phase. Row of buildings in center of the picture is part of the field built in 1917. Beyond the buildings, in the left upper half of the photo, is the Village of Rantoul. This picture also gives a good view of White Hall, the enormous building behind the hangars. USAF

while, facilities deteriorated due to the lack of adequate funding. The students were hampered by poor living conditions and inadequate facilities. One local paper commenting on the living conditions at Chanute in 1931 said, "It is doubtful if there is a penal institution in Illinois with such poorly constructed quarters as those at Chanute Field in which are quartered the men on whom the country is to rely in time of conflict." It went on to say, "Chanute Field buildings are of flimsy, wartime construction. They were erected at a time when the country was confronted by an emergency and when speed of construction meant everything. Everything at the Field was temporary."

During the mid-thirties, the Air Corps was expanding. It was becoming clear that Chanute could not handle the need to train the additional mechanics and technicians because of the field's inadequate facilities. There was much pressure to either rebuild the school or move it to another site. Many politicians favored moving the school to Denver, Colorado. However, in 1936, Congress voted to keep the field at Chanute. In 1937, some training responsibility was moved to Lowry Field in Denver to provide more space for the training of mechanics. But, the inadequate and poorly funded facilities remained. The issue was resolved in 1938, when funding was provided to rebuild the outdated and deteriorating airfield. This building program created today's Chanute Air Force Base. It would serve the country in World War II, Korea, Vietnam, and throughout the Cold War by providing the highly trained technicians and specialists necessary for a successful military force.

When the rebuilding of the field started in 1938, it was nothing more than a run-down facility consisting of old wooden buildings, with a grass airfield, some aircraft, and about 1,000 unhappy men. Officers and enlisted men sent to the field considered it a trip to Siberia. Some officers sent here were those who were not well thought of by the Air Corps. It would be their last stop before leaving the service. The saying in the Air Corps at the time was "don't shoot 'em, Chanute 'em." The saying not only referred to the run-down facilities, but also the location, said to be in the middle of a corn field far removed from any major population centers. This would change in the three years it took to rebuild the field. Chanute would soon become one of the world's best training facilities. A new headquarters was built along with massive hangars, a hospital, warehouses, barracks, officer quarters, engine test buildings, family housing, a gymnasium, and concrete runways. About $14 million was spent, most of it through the Works Progress Administration (WPA). Most of the buildings were of permanent construction, and they remain today. Some housing and major buildings, i.e., hospital, administration, were of red brick colonial-style construction. Today, they sit in an almost park-like setting, on quiet streets lined with the oak trees planted at the time. The school buildings are also of permanent construction and with their tree-shaded lawns the area looks more like a college campus than a military base. The largest building built was White Hall, known as "Buckingham Palace." It was designed to house 2,200 men and contained its own mess hall, barber shop, and post exchange. At the time, it was the largest military building in the United States. Construction was finished in mid-1941, about six months before Pearl Harbor.

With the war, the demand for trained personnel soon grew beyond Chanute's ability to handle the requirement. The basic aircraft mechanic's course was shifted to Lincoln Field, Nebraska, and Seymour Johnson Field, in North Carolina, when these new fields were ready. Chanute would train men in advanced and specialized mechanics courses, maintenance engineering, instruments, propellers, power plant operations, sheet metal work, welding, link trainer instruction, control tower operation, teletype maintenance, weather, and cryptography. The field was overcrowded and reached a peak student load of 25,000 in January 1943. New temporary barracks were built, but there still was not enough room. Some soldiers lived in tents. Flying training was also done at Chanute; however, it was never of the intensity or scope of the training fields built for this purpose. Four-engine training started in September 1943 with the B-17, but by spring 1944, training had shifted to the B-25. Fixed-wing aviation training stopped in September 1944 when the training unit was transferred to Courtland Army Air Base in Alabama. During 1940 to 1945, more than 200,000 men and women received training and graduated from the many courses taught at the field.

The 99th Pursuit Squadron, the Army Air Forces first all-black fighter squadron, was activated at Chanute Field in March 1941. Here the aircraft mechanics, clerks, and others learned their trade before being sent to Maxwell Field, Alabama, in October 1941, and later to Tuskeegee, Alabama. The first six black aviation cadets were also trained at Chanute, some in armament, others in communications or mechanics. These men also worked with the enlisted members of the 99th, helping them learn military drill. Pilots for the 99th were trained at Moton Field and Sharps Field near Tuskeegee, Alabama.

With the end of the war, Chanute became a separation center, the second largest in the Army Air Forces, and discharged more than 30,000 troops before the center was closed in January 1946. Early in the same year, the student population was less than 5,000. The school was now teaching jet propulsion technical training and, with just 5,000 students, the base seemed empty. Some excess barracks space was used by the University of Illinois for a short time to house war veterans attending the university. But because of the distance from the school, it was stopped after one semester.

Jet propulsion training graduated about 2,000 jet engine mechanics in 1948 and this course remained as one of the major subjects taught at the school. Again, as funding declined, the base started to deteriorate and by 1949 it was in major disrepair. By September 1950, the student population had dropped to 2,450 students. With the Korean war, the load again picked up, and by 1953 there were over 11,000 students on base. Also, the Base Commander, Brigadier General Byron Gates, who assumed command in 1949, was working wonders improving the conditions at the field. Much of the improvement was accomplished by the students waiting to enter training. New dormitories were built and "Buckingham Palace" was converted into classrooms. General Gates' tour would be the longest of any Chanute commander (1949–1955). During this time, he made a major contribution bringing the base up to Air Force standards and in improving relations with the community.

With the arrival of the Cold War, Chanute became involved in training maintenance personnel to maintain the Strategic Air Command's bombers and missiles. Thousands were trained to maintain the various models of the B-52 along with other courses related to the huge bomber. The field also supplied trained personnel for many other aircraft, including the F-111, B-58, KC-135, and the B-1. As the Air Force became involved with the missile program, Chanute would provide the training necessary to maintain and launch the new weapons. By 1958, the field had courses that provided training on nine different missile systems. By 1959, this had grown to 33 different courses. To support its increasing role in missile personnel training, additional facilities were constructed. Also, in 1964, Chanute began instruction in the basics of aircraft and structural fire fighting. Over time, the field became the free world's most complete fire protection training center. By 1967, fifty years after the opening of the field, Chanute had trained 1,000,000 students. This included pilots, navigators, and bombardiers. Students were also trained in gunnery, parachuting, aerial photography, maintenance, technicians, and maintenance management. Aircraft ranged from the Curtiss JN-4 Jenny through the B-36 to the MX missile. By 1971, Chanutes flying mission ended with the closing of the runways.

In the late seventies, training continued on both missiles, Air Launched Cruise Missiles, and the new engines used in the F-15 and F-16 along with other projects. In 1979, the field was designated the prime training center for the Advanced Intercontinental Ballistic Missile System. In the early Eighties additional construction gave the field a new Visiting Officers Quarters, an Arts and Crafts Center, and a three million-dollar gymnasium. A new shopping center complex was opened that included a Base Exchange, Commissary, Bowling Center, Post Office, and Airmen's Center. Additional housing was built and in late 1986 a $6 million Fire Protection Training Complex was completed. A 100-acre recreation park was built in 1987, which included facilities for fishing, picnicking, and camping.

By the late eighties and early nineties, the field had added a Fuel Training Complex, expanded the Jet Engine Training Facility, and had a new Weather Training Complex. This was just after completing another major renovation to the field. Chanute ranked among the best of the Air Force Bases in terms of training capability and living facilities for its airmen and their families. Unfortunately, the Department of Defense decided it was time to close the base and 85 others over the next five years to save defense dollars. The base closed on September 30, 1993. Chanute Air Force Base was the Air Force's oldest Technical Training Center, the third most senior active Air Force base, and served for over 75 years. Chanute trained over 2,000,000 people. Their skills helped the Air Force keep the peace through the Cold War and win the skies in two World Wars, Korea, Vietnam and many other smaller but deadly conflicts.

Today's entrance to the former air base. The structure, a former gate house, has been removed. THOLE

The Command Center building for Chanute Air Force Base. This was one of the structures built by the WPA during the expansion of 1938. THOLE

Interior view of the staircase in the command center building. Note the stainless steel stair railing with the art deco design. THOLE

The base hospital built during the 1938 expansion. It was used as a hospital until 1957 when a new hospital was constructed. THOLE

Interior view of a hallway in the former base hospital. After the new hospital opened in 1957, the building was used for office space and perhaps classrooms. THOLE

A view of the four hangars in 1995. The smallest hangar is in the foreground, while the roof of the fourth hangar can be seen over the top of the smallest one. Note the size of the hangars in relation to the aircraft. THOLE

A side view of a hangar.
THOLE

Interior view of one of the larger hangars. This shows about one third of the space in the hangar. At the time it was being used by an auto company to store parts.
THOLE

A former USAF Connie awaits its fate. The building behind was used as the weather school; about half of the building is visible.
THOLE

Officer housing along one of the residential streets of the former air base. These homes were part of the 1938 expansion construction. THOLE

This shows a side view of the former base hospital, built in 1957. THOLE

A partial view of White Hall, constructed in the late thirties expansion. During WW II, it was used to house about 2,200 soldiers. Following the war, it was converted into classrooms. THOLE

One of the modern-day buildings, the former base Commissary. THOLE

This is one of the few remaining World War II era buildings left on the former base. THOLE

Swimming pool located behind the former officers club. THOLE

Painting on the interior wall of one of the classroom buildings. They were typically done by students and often were signed with their class number. THOLE

Exterior view of one set of the jet engine test cells. There were two complexes like this designed to instruct jet engine technicians. THOLE

A partial view of "Pace-setter Park." A 100-acre outdoor recreation area for the families of the men and women stationed at Chanute. Today it is used by the Village of Rantoul for the same purpose. THOLE

Mathies Hall, a former dormitory, now in use by a trucking company to house its students. THOLE

This sign posted on the former dental clinic entrance says it all. THOLE

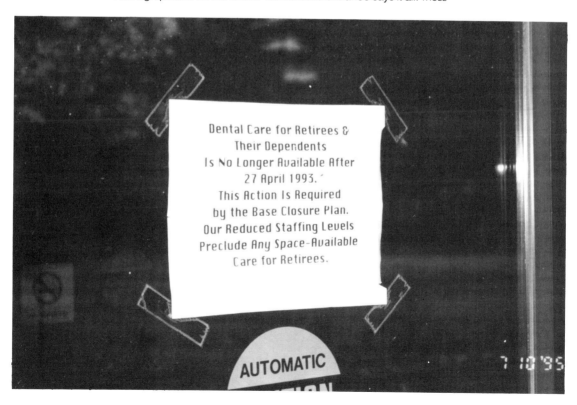

Dental Care for Retirees &
Their Dependents
Is No Longer Available After
27 April 1993.
This Action Is Required
by the Base Closure Plan.
Our Reduced Staffing Levels
Preclude Any Space-Available
Care for Retirees.

FROM B-24s TO P-38s

....

Ephrata Army Air Base

IN 1934, EPHRATA Army Air Base was a small local airport with two dirt landing strips; however, by 1942, it was a major Army Air Forces training field with over 1,000 buildings. Four years later, it was semi-abandoned and fighting to retain its usefulness. Today, not much is left to remind the visitor of its proud role in the training of bomber crews and fighter pilots during the war.

During the thirties, the field grew with the help of government funds. By 1935, it had a lighted beacon, a 24-hour radio station, and runway border lights. The radio station broadcasted Morse code to help guide pilots and, with its lighted beacon, the field became a safe haven for pilots unable to land at other airports because of weather problems. As an example, in early 1937 two Northwest Airlines planes landed at Ephrata because of poor weather at Spokane. Ephrata was far off the beaten path. The field lies in central Washington State, 130 air miles east of Seattle and about 100 miles west of Spokane. The town's population in 1940 was around 300. The airport sits in flat semi-arid country; bitterly cold in winter and extremely hot, dusty, and windy in the summer.

As early as 1934, the Ephrata Chamber of Commerce was active in attempting to get the Army Air Corps interested in establishing an aerodrome near the town. Repeated requests and proposals submitted over the years generated little interest by the War Department and the Air Corps. However, by 1940, the world situation had changed. It was becoming clear the United States might find itself involved in a war no one wanted. Worst of all, the U.S. was unprepared to defend itself. The Congress was starting to realize this and funds were now being allocated to build up the armed forces that had fallen into a terrible state of neglect. The Air Corps, soon to become the Army Air Forces, was now interested in any reasonable proposal that would help ease the incredible training responsibility being thrust upon it. Hundreds of new training fields were urgently needed to train the thousands of new pilots, navigators, and bomb aimers necessary to fight a war.

In 1939, the Chamber of Commerce made another presentation to General H. H. Arnold (head of the Air Corps) however it was again turned down. But, several months later, another request was submitted and after a favorable report about the site by Major Peck of the Spokane National Guard Squadron, the site was approved. By this time, 1940, the airport had 2,560 acres available for development with about 320 more, if needed. The land would be leased to the government.

The improvements made at Ephrata were piecemeal, primarily because it was not originally intended to serve as a training field. By March 1941, bombing ranges were being established near the field and the first major upgrade to the airport was announced in April 1941. Works Projects Administration funds (a depression-era program) were used to paint buildings, install a revolving beacon, and improve the phone system between the Seattle Traffic Control Center and aircraft. Up to this point, all construction and improvements at the field were made for civilian use; however, during and following these improvements the field would be used as a base of operations for the bombers and crews using the newly established and nearby bombing ranges. They were located about 20 miles from the aerodrome. But, no provisions were made for the numerous men and planes operating out of the base. By November 1941, the Work Projects Administration improvements were completed, but the field still did not have a paved runway. Bids for one concrete runway were let on December 5, 1941. Two days later, the United States was involved in a World War.

The Second Air Force had responsibility for training in the western part of the country, but as late as January 1942, the Second Air Force had only four training fields. Ephrata was still being used as a support base for the nearby bombing ranges, but did not have a paved runway until April. Personnel and equipment to support the facility were scattered between the airfield and the town. Facilities were virtually nonexistent. Most of the support personnel lived in the town in tents. Some old Civilian Conservation Corps buildings (another depression-era project) were found and used for the bombing range headquarters, offices, a post exchange, and infirmary. Seriously ill patients had to be transported to Spokane about 100 miles away. One visitor to the base in early June 1942, remembers it as having a nice long runway, one or two buildings, and tents. This changed by mid-June when the field was designated the home for the 307th Bomb Group and officially recognized as Ephrata Army Air Base. Pandemonium was about to break loose.

Over the next few months, thousands of airmen and support personnel descended upon the barren base set out in the middle of nowhere. Tents went up everywhere. There were no buildings, warehouses, or a hospital. Supplies were left in the open and guarded. Refrigerated rail cars were used to store food and a hospital in Soap Lake (about five miles away) was leased to provide medical care. The warehouse space that was available in the town of Ephrata was rented to store supplies. Dust and dirt were everywhere and sanitation facilities were virtually nonexistent. There were no facilities to launder clothing, so local laundries were used. More abandoned Civilian Conservation Corps buildings were found and transported to the base. They were converted into badly needed offices, warehouses, and other type buildings. Meanwhile, the soldiers continued to live in six-man tents without floors. A post engineer was not assigned until August. Morale was low, and AWOLs were high.

In June 1942, Ephrata's mission changed when it was decided to bring the base up to the standards of full-fledged training field. This meant construct-

ing semi-permanent buildings, called "Theater of Operations" type. The buildings were single story and generally made of wood with a tar-paper siding. They were set on a poured concrete foundation or on concrete blocks. Heat was supplied by a coal burning stove located in the middle of the building. The buildings were bitterly cold in the winter and hot and dusty in the summer; however, to the men at Ephrata, who were used to living in tents, the buildings were a magnificent improvement. Some other structures such as the hospital, auditorium, the gymnasium, and the civilian dorm were of the "Mobilization" type. This was a more permanent and comfort-

The Ephrata Army Air Base cantonment area as it appeared in 1947. Silo type buildings to the right rear of hangar no. 2 are Celestial Navigation Trainer buildings.
SPOKESMAN REVIEW VIA DUNSTON COLLECTION

able building, often two stories high, with central heating. A sewage system was installed, doing away with the primitive latrines. Water was piped in and permanent roads were put down. A non-commissioned officers club was built, along with a chapel, and a base theater. Most of this construction was not completed until September 1943. By then, the field had three runways. In October, a new hospital with 300 beds was opened. Unique to Ephrata was the enlisted men's living quarters. Instead of the standard barracks-type buildings, a smaller building called a "hutment" was used. Typically, they were about 16 feet square, with two windows and were heated by a stove in the center of the room. Double-deck bunk beds were placed around the four walls. They were built to house six men, but often slept as many as twelve. The hutments were built on wood skids and could be moved at will. The base had over 1,000 buildings, about 800 were hutments.

Ephrata Army Air Base trained both individuals and entire bomb groups at one time or another. Some groups that trained or served at the base included, the 307th Bomb Group, the 304th Bomb Group (later renamed the 2nd Bomb Group), the 95th Bomb Group, the 381st Bomb Group, and a squadron of the 34th Bomb Group. Later, the 395th Bomb Group was formed as an operational training unit. It supplied personnel to the newly activated 401st and 447th Bomb Groups. In September 1943, the 483rd Bomb Group was activated. The 457th trained here before leaving in December. Both B-17s and B-24s were used at Ephrata. The gunnery and bombing ranges were located near the base and used by the groups and individuals being trained. One former airman recalls, "I fondly remember a gunnery training school near Soap Lake. It was in a wide canyon. The camp was primarily tents and some gunnery ranges with the canyon walls as back stops for the machine gun fire. By raising the guns high enough, we could see the sun reflect off of the copper jacket slugs in flight. I recall the camp must have been a few miles out of town . . . We lived in tents behind the building for one or two weeks and that was all. The gunnery ranges were across the road. Some of them were just .30 and .50 caliber machine guns fixed on posts. One of the more interesting arrangements was a jeep with a fifth wheel fixed on a boom in front, which guided the jeep by means of a wooden rail around an oval path. The jeep carried a target above it. We fired the .50 caliber machine guns while tracking the jeep target. The jeep was well protected by earthen barriers. We made

Aerial view of Ephrata Army
Air Base, 1994. Note resur-
faced north/south runway.
PORT OF EPHRATA VIA DUNSTON
COLLECTION

355th Squadron area show-
ing orderly, supply, and day
room in the foreground. In
the background are the
machine shop, the para-
chute building, and a large
hangar, 1943. Note the
rather bleak appearance of
the base. Ephrata probably
suffered from having a
series of different missions
and organizations during its
wartime use. There wasn't
time for an organization to
take ownership of the post
and develop pride in its
appearance, as in many
other temporary training
fields. USAF VIA DUNSTON
COLLECTION

A composite picture of the
355th Squadron area. This
gives a good view of the Six
Man Hutments. The large
building to the right rear is a
mess hall, 1943. USAF VIA
DUNSTON COLLECTION

P-39s undergoing production line maintenance, 1944. Aircraft seems unusually dirty, even for a trainer.
USAF VIA DUNSTON COLLECTION

Interior view of a service club, 1943. USAF VIA DUNSTON COLLECTION

every effort to hit the jeep but were unsuccessful. When it was not used as a target, we would ride on the jeep around the track."

The 457th was the last bomb group to train at Ephrata, and after leaving in December 1943, the base was empty except for the personnel necessary to maintain the facilities on a standby basis. During April 1944, the Fourth Air Force took over Ephrata for fighter pilot training. By this time the field was a reasonably comfortable station. The major task necessary to bring the facility up to training status was to clean buildings that had not been used for

three months, and replace equipment taken by the departing units.

Parts of the 478th Fighter Group and the 473rd Fighter Group moved onto the field. Flying training began with the P-39 on April 16, 1944. When the pilots arrived at Ephrata they had completed primary, basic and advanced training, received their wings, and were commissioned officers. The next step was to learn to fly the planes they would use in combat. For the first three months the P-39 fighter was used for training. Harry Tyndale, Class 44 B, remembers the P-39 fondly and writes, "The greatest,

The hospital complex, circa 1947. At the time, it was being used as living quarters for people employed by the Bureau of Reclamation for the Columbia Basin Irrigation project. PORT OF EPHRATA VIA DUNSTON COLLECTION

wildest flying of my life—in the slickest little fighter ever made . . . My tour was the greatest, most memorable flying experience that I've ever been engaged in. We were flying P-39s then . . . The P-38 was not the kick that the P-39 in the deserts of Central Washington was. We used to fly them down the canyons, we rat-raced every day, it was just the greatest, most thrilling type of flying that I was ever engaged in." Later in July, P-63s began to replace the obsolete P-39s. The conversion was completed by September. Beginning October, 1944, another training change was made for the trainees to receive both first- and second-phase training at the base. When this training was completed, they were qualified for assignment to a combat ready unit. The P-38 was used for this training and about 120 flying hours were allocated. Gorden Fuqua remembers the training schedule in effect at the time, "Normally we flew in the morning and attended ground school in the afternoon one week, and reversed the procedure the following week . . . Of course, we couldn't fly every day because of factors such as weather, more students than aircraft, and various other reasons . . . Instrument training requires a specified amount of time in Link trainers and a specified amount of time actually flying aircraft on instruments. Most instrument flying in actual aircraft was accomplished in BT-13s to have a second pilot as observer (for safety reasons). However, some of our instrument flying was accomplished in the fighter aircraft, with a second aircraft flying alongside as lookout. Blind Flying in a P-38 is a pretty sporty experience."

Class 44 E was the last to train at Ephrata. Training activity was gradually phased out and by February 1945 the base was a ghost town with only a small number of personnel remaining as caretakers. Notices began to appear in the newspaper that buildings from the base and the nearby bombing ranges were to be sold; however, the situation again changed in July 1945, with the arrival of almost 2,000 members from the East Coast Training Command. They descended upon an empty base ill prepared to meet their needs. The reason for the influx of new personnel was the build up of trained B-24 crews for the invasion of Japan.

With the surrender of Japan, there was no need for the aircraft or crews; however, personnel continued to pour into Ephrata. By this time, there were 40 to 50 B-24s on the base. Flying continued so the men could earn flight pay and to keep them occupied while they were being processed. By October, Ephrata was designated a sub-base of McChord Army

Air Field. Again the base was slowly shut down, so that by the end of November 1945, only a few service personnel remained on the field. For a while, the former air field was used as a staging point for construction work on dams and irrigation canals for the Columbia Basin Project. The buildings were used for apartments, dormitories, warehouses, and office space. Eight hundred of the hutments were moved to provide housing at other Bureau of Reclamation projects. The chapel was moved from the field into Ephrata and is now the Memorial Christian Church. A plaque honoring the men and women who served at the former air base has been placed in the Chapel's entry.

Today, there is not much left of the former air base to remind one of its war time service. Some buildings remain, including two hangars, a few warehouses near the railroad tracks, and the old gymnasium. Walking along the grounds, the visitor will notice some building foundations slowly being covered with weeds and brush; however, the former airfield is far from deserted. Significant improvements have been made over the years to encourage business growth and improve the quality of the field. Today, the airport is used by both private and corporate aircraft, and the former cantonment area is being developed for industrial and commercial use. An agricultural sprayer company operates from the airport along with an Alaska Air Freight maintenance facility. Also the field has become known as "The Soaring Capital of the Northwest" because of its fine thermal conditions. There are four glider clubs at the airport, and the weekends are quite busy with sailplane activity. National and regional glider contests are held here. Also, yearly competitions sponsored by the International Aerobatics Club with powered aircraft take place at Ephrata. The city and county have further development plans and the future of the former airbase looks bright.

Hangar 1 on left, and hangar 2 as they appeared in 1995. DUNSTON

Rear view of same hangars. Sloped concrete slab in foreground of picture is the foundation for the former base theater. DUNSTON

The gymnasium, has been refurbished, and is now used by a local gymnastics club. DUNSTON

A 1995 view of the former parachute loft. Here parachutes were unpacked and hung on a scheduled basis in the taller structure to prevent formation of mildew. Then they would be repacked and reissued.
DUNSTON

This was the bomb trainer building, now used for airport maintenance. DUNSTON

A close-up rear view of hangar 1. It's used by a steel fabricating business and has been resided. DUNSTON

This tower held the revolving beacon first installed by the CAA (forerunner of today's FAA) in 1941. The revolving beacon was replaced by a strobe light in 1995. Behind the tower is the bomb sight storage building, and the bomb trainer building. DUNSTON

The bomb sight storage building as it appears today. During WW II, the then secret Norden Bomb Sights were guarded 24 hours a day, and when not in use, kept secured in buildings like this. DUNSTON

· · ·

The former hospital mess hall, since refurbished and now used by the "Wheatland Whirlers," a square dance club. DUNSTON

A good view of today's flight line that shows hangars 1 & 2 along with the beacon tower. DUNSTON

The base chapel as it appeared in 1995. It was moved about a mile from the airfield and is still in use today, little changed from its war time service except for the addition of the cross and vestibule. DUNSTON

. . .

A 1993 view of former Ephrata Army Air Base warehouses sitting along side of their spur track. DUNSTON

Foundation remains of a former Celestial Navigation Trainer. DUNSTON

Remains of a cinder "sidewalk" that was once around the bomb group hutment area. DUNSTON

These rocks were lined up against a hutment, and today outline where it once stood. DUNSTON

APPENDIX

······································

USAAF Airfields

NAME OF FIELD/AIRSTRIP	MILES AND DIRECTION FROM NEAREST CITY/TOWN

ALABAMA

Anniston Army Air Field	15 mi. SW Anniston
Auburn-Opelika	3 mi. E Auburn
Autaugaville (Craig Field, aux.)	20 mi. W Selma
Bates Field (ASC)	10 mi. W Mobile
Birmingham Army Air Field	5 mi. NE Birmingham
Brockley Field (ASC)	4 mi. S Mobile
Camp Sibert Army Air Field	3 mi. S Attala
Courtland Army Air Field	1 mi. SW Courtland
Craig Field	5 mi. SE Selma
Dannelly Field	8 mi. SW Montgomery
Demopolis Airfield (Key Field, aux.)	8 mi. WSW Demopolis
Dothan	2 mi. WNW Dothan
Elmore (Gunter Field, aux.)	10 mi. N Montgomery
Furniss (Craig Field, aux.)	10 mi. SSW Selma
Gunter Field	2 mi. NE Montgomery
Henderson (Craig Field, aux.)	29 mi. SW Selma
Huntsville Arsenal Field	7 mi. SW Huntsville
Maxwell Field	2 mi. W Montgomery
Mollette (Craig Field, aux.)	16 mi. SSW Selma
Muscle Shoals	1 mi. E Muscle Shoals
Napier Field	7 mi. NW Dothan
Ozark Army Air Field	12 mi. SSW Ozark
Roberts (Gliders only)	8 mi. NNW Birmingham
Selfield Field	4 mi. ENE Selma
St. Elmo Municipal Airport (ASC)	St. Elmo
Tuskegee Army Air Field	7 mi. NW Tuskegee
Tuskegee Institute #1	4 mi. SSE Tuskegee
Tuskegee Institute #2	3 mi. N Tuskegee

ARIZONA

Ajo Army Air Field	6 mi. N Ajo
Coolidge Army Air Field	7 mi. SE Coolidge
Datelan Army Air Field	2 mi. NE Datelan
Davis-Monthan Field	4 mi. SE Tucson
Douglas Army Air Field	8 mi. NNW Douglas
Forrest aux. #2 (Douglas AAF, aux.)	6 mi. WNW Douglas
Gila Bend Army Air Field	4 mi. S Gila Bend
Gila Bend aux. #1	15 mi. SW Gila Bend
Gila Bend aux. #2	18 mi. SSW Gila Bend
Gila Bend aux. #3	8 mi. WSW Gila Bend
Hereford Army Air Field	1 mi. WNW Hereford
Kingman Army Air Field	3 mi. NE Kingman
Earnest Love Field	8 mi. NNE Prescott

Luke Field	15 mi. WSW Phoenix
Laguna Landing Strip	6 mi. NE Laguna
McNeal aux. #1 (Douglas AAF, aux.)	Douglas
Marana Army Air Field	8 mi. NW Marana
Safford Field	6 mi. ENE Safford
Sahuarita Flight Strip	2 mi. E Sahuarita
Sky Harbor Airport (ATC)	2 mi. E Phoenix
Tucson Municipal Airport	6 mi. S Tucson
Williams Field	9 mi. E Chandler
Winslow Municipal Airport (ATC)	2 mi. SW Winslow
Yucca Army Air Field	1 mi. NE Yucca
Yuma Army Air Field	2 mi. S Yuma

ARKANSAS

Adams Field (ATC)	2 mi. SE Little Rock
Blytheville Army Air Field	2 mi. NW Blytheville
Carlisle (Stuttgart AAF, aux.)	26 mi. NW Stuttgart
Cooter (Blytheville AAF, aux.)	10 mi. NE Blytheville
Hazen (Stuttgart AAF, aux.)	19 mi. NNW Stuttgart
Hope Army Air Field	3 mi. NE Hope
Manila (Blytheville AAF, aux.)	13 mi. W Blytheville
Newport Army Air Field	6 mi. NE Newport
Praireville (Stuttgart AAF, aux.)	8 mi. SE Stuttgart
Steele (Blytheville AAF, aux.)	12 mi. N Blytheville
Stuttgart Army Air Field	6 mi. N Stuttgart
Walnut Ridge Army Air Base	4 mi. NE Walnut Ridge

CALIFORNIA

Allen (Gardner Field aux.)	25 mi. SE Taft
Bakersfield Municipal Airport	4 mi. NW Bakersfield
Banning Landing Strip	1 mi. SE Banning
Bidwell Field	2 mi. SW Red Bluff
Bishop Army Air Field	2 mi. NE Bishop
Blythe Army Air Field	7 mi. W Blythe
Camp Kearney NAAS	9 mi. N San Diego
Chico Army Air Field	5 mi. NE Chico
Clover Field	3 mi. E Santa Monica
Concord Army Air Field	1 mi. NW Concord
Daggett Municipal Airport	6 mi. E Daggett
Delano Army Air Field	1 mi. S Delano
Desert Center Army Air Field	2 mi. NE Desert Center
Eagle Field	6 mi. SW Dos Palos
Estrella Army Air Field	5 mi. NE Paso Robles

NAME OF FIELD/AIRSTRIP	MILES AND DIRECTION FROM NEAREST CITY/TOWN	NAME OF FIELD/AIRSTRIP	MILES AND DIRECTION FROM NEAREST CITY/TOWN
Eureka Navy Airport	14 mi. N Eureka	Salinas Army Air Base	3 mi. SE Salinas
Fairfield-Suisun Army Air Field	5 mi. E Fairfield	San Bernardino Army Air Depot	3 mi. ESE San Bernardino
Gardner Field	8 mi. E Gardner	San Diego Municipal Airport	1 mi. W San Diego
Grand Central Air Terminal		San Diego Naval Air Station	North Island
(March Field, sub base)	6 mi. NW Glendale	San Nicolas Army Air Field	75 mi. SW Los Angeles
Half Moon Bay Flight Strip	5 mi. NW Half Moon Bay	Santa Maria Army Air Field	4 mi. S Santa Maria
Hamilton Field	7 mi. NNE San Rafiel	Santa Rosa Army Air Field	7 mi. NW Santa Rosa
Hammer Field	5 mi. NE Fresno	Shaver's Summitt Field	30 mi. ESE Indio
Hayward Army Air Field	3 mi. W Hayward	Siskiyou County Field	5 mi. NE Montaque
Hawthorne Field	1 mi. E Hawthorne	Stockton Field	4 mi. SSE Stockton
Kern (Gardner Field, aux.)	21 mi. SE Taft	Thermal Army Air Field	2 mi. SW Thermal
Kern County Field	1 mi. WNW Inyokern	Victorville Army Air Field	5 mi. NW Victorville
Kern County Field	5 mi. NNW Bakersfield	Visalia Army Air Field	6 mi. W Visalia
Kearney-Mesa Airport	8 mi. NE San Diego	Willows Airfield (Hamilton	
King City Field	2 mi. NNE King City	Field, aux.)	1 mi. W Willows
Lemoore Army Air Field	9 mi. SW Lemoore	Winters Flight Strip	7 mi. NE Winters
Lindbergh	2 mi. W San Diego	Van Nuys Metro Airport	17 mi. NW Los Angeles
Lomita Flight Strip	1 mi. W Lomita		
Long Beach Army Air Field (ATC)	4 mi. NE Long Beach	**COLORADO**	
Los Angeles Field	11 mi. SW Los Angeles		
Lost Hills-Kern County	1 mi. NE Lost Hills	Arlington (La Junta, aux.)	28 mi. NNE Arlington
March Field	10 mi. SE Riverside	Buckley Field	8 mi. SE Denver
Marysville Army Air Field	3 mi. S Marysville	Denver Municipal Airport	5 mi. ENE Denver
Mather Field	10 mi. E Sacramento	La Junta Army Air Field	4 mi. NNE La Junta
M C Flight Test Base	20 mi. SE Mojave	Las Animas (La Junta, aux.)	19 mi. NE La Junta
McClellan Field	8 mi. NE Sacramento	Leadville Flight Strip	2 mi. W Leadville
Merced Army Air Field	6 mi. NW Merced	Lowry Field	1 mi. SE Denver
Merced Air Base (Merced AAF, aux.)	2 mi. NW Merced	Peterson Field	7 mi. ESE Colorado
Metropolitan Airport	2 mi. NW Van Nuys		Springs
Mills Field	10 mi. S San Francisco	Pueblo Army Air Base	7 mi. ENE Pueblo
Mines Field	10 mi. SW Los Angeles	Pueblo Field	2 mi. SW Pueblo
Minter Field	14 mi. NW Bakersfield	Rocky Ford (La Junta, aux.)	14 mi. NW La Junta
Modesto Field	2 mi. ESE Modesto		
Montague Airfield	3 mi. NE Montague	**CONNECTICUT**	
Muroc Army Air Field	1 mi. S Muroc		
Muroc Flight Test Base	3 mi. N Muroc	Bradley Field	2 mi. W Windsor Locks
Napa Airfield	5 mi. S Napa	Brainard Field	2 mi. SSE Hartford
Needles Army Airfield	5 mi. S Needles	Bridgeport Army Air Field	3 mi. SE Stratford
Oakland Municipal Airport		Groton Army Air Field	3 mi. SE Groton
(Hamilton Field, sub base)	5 mi. S Oakland	New Haven Army Air Field	3 mi. SE New Haven
Ontario Army Air Field	1 mi. E Ontario	Rentschler Field	3 mi. ESE Hartford
Orange County Army Air Field	4 mi. S Santa Ana		
Oroville Army Air Field	3 mi. SW Oroville	**DELAWARE**	
Otay-Mesa NAAS	14 mi. SE San Diego		
Oxnard Flight Strip	6 mi. E Oxnard	Dover Army Air Field	4 mi. SE Dover
Palmdale Army Air Field	3 mi. NE Palmdale	New Castle Army Air Base	5 mi. SW Wilmington
Palm Springs Army Air Field	2 mi. E Palm Springs		
Parker (Gardner Field aux.)	15 mi. SE Taft	**FLORIDA**	
Potterville Army Air Field	3 mi. SW Potterville		
Ream Field (March Field, aux.)	12 mi. S San Diego	Alachua Army Air Field	3 mi. NE Gainesville
Redding Army Air Field	7 mi. SE Redding	Apalachicola Army Air Field	8 mi. W Apalachicola
Rice Army Air Field	2 mi. ESE Rice	Avon Park Army Air Field	10 mi. ENE Avon Park
Sacramento Municipal Airport		Bartow Army Air Field	5 mi. NE Bartow
(Hamilton Field, sub base)	5 mi. S Sacramento	Boca Raton Army Air Field	2 mi. NW Boca Raton
		Brooksville Army Air Field	10 mi. S Brooksville
		Buckingham Army Air Field	4 mi. E Fort Myers
		Bushnell Army Air Field	3 mi. NE Bushnell

· · ·

NAME OF FIELD/AIRSTRIP	MILES AND DIRECTION FROM NEAREST CITY/TOWN	NAME OF FIELD/AIRSTRIP	MILES AND DIRECTION FROM NEAREST CITY/TOWN
Carrabelle Flight Strip	2 mi. W Carrabelle	Bush Field	8 mi. SSE Augusta
Cross City Army Air Field	1 mi. E Cross City	Bainbridge Army Air Field	4 mi. NNW Bainbridge
Dale Mabry Field	2 mi. WSW Tallahassee	Bemis Field (Moody Field, aux.)	12 mi. NE Valdosta
Drew Field	5 mi. W Tampa	Camp Stewart Army Air Field	3 mi. NE Hinesville
Dunnellon Army Air	5 mi. E Dunnellon	Chatham Army Air Field	6 mi. NW Savannah
Elgin Field	2 mi. W Valpariso	Cochran Field	9 mi. S Macon
Elgin Aux. #1	14 mi. NNE Valpariso	Commodre Decatur Field	2 mi. W Bainbridge
Elgin Aux. #2	6 mi. NNE Valpariso	Cordele Field	2 mi. NNE Cordele
Elgin Aux. #3	10 mi. N Valpariso	Daniel Field	3 mi. WSW Augusta
Elgin Aux. #4	6 mi. W Valpariso	Dublin Airfield	5 mi. NW Dublin
Elgin Aux. #5	10 mi. NW Valpariso	Harris Neck Army Air Field	7 mi. E S. Newport
Elgin Aux. #6	18 mi. WNW Valpariso	Herbert Smart Airport	4 mi. E Macon
Elgin Aux. #7	19 mi. W Valpariso	Homerville Flight Strip	2 mi. NW Homerville
Elgin Aux. #8	10 mi. ENE Valpariso	Hunter Field	3 mi. SW Savannah
Elgin Aux. #9	14 mi. WSW Valpariso	Lake Park Field (Moody Field, aux.)	12 mi. SSE Valdosta
Hendricks Field	5 mi. SE Sebring	Lawson Field	8 mi. S Columbus
Hillsborough Army Air Field	6 mi. NNW Tampa	Marietta Army Air Field	2 mi. SE Marietta
Homestead Army Air Field	5 mi. ENE Homestead	Moody Field	12 mi. NE Valdosta
Immokalee Airfield	1 mi. NE Immokalee	Moultrie Field	7 mi. S Moultrie
Jacksonville Army Air Field	6 mi. N Jacksonville	Robins Field	17 mi. SE Macon
Keystone Army Air Field	3 mi. NNW Keystone Heights	Spence Field	4 mi. SE Moultrie
		Statesboro Army Air Field	3 mi. NE Statesboro
Kissimmee Army Air Field	2 mi. N Kissimmee	Sylvania Army Air Field	7 mi. SSE Sylvania
Lakeland Army Air Field	5 mi. SW Lakeland	Thomasville Army Air Field	8 mi. NE Thomasville
Lakeland Field	3 mi. N Lakeland	Tifton Field	2 mi. SE Tifton
Lake Wales Airfield	2 mi. WSW Lake Wales	Turner Field	3 mi. E Albany
Leesburg Army Air Field	5 mi. E Leesburg	Valdosta Field	2 mi. S Valdosta
Leesburg Base Services	7 mi. NW Leesburg	Vidalia Airfield	3 mi. SE Vidalia
Mac Dill Field	8 mi. SSW Tampa	Waycross Army Air Field	3 mi. NW Waycross
Marathon Flight Strip	3 mi. ENE Marathon		
Marianna Army Air Field	6 mi. NNE Marianna		

IDAHO

Montbrook Army Air Field	2 mi. NW Montbrook	Gowen Field	3 mi. S Boise
Morrison Field	2 mi. SW Palm Beach	Mountain Home Army Air Base	11 mi. WSW Mountain Home
Naples Army Air Field	1 mi. NE Naples		
Orlando Air Base	2 mi. E Orlando	Pocatello Army Air Field	8 mi. NW Pocatello
Page Field	4 mi. S Fort Myers	Pocatello Field	6 mi. NW Pocatello
Palm Beach County Park	2 mi. WNW Lantana		
Pan American 36th St., Army Air Base	6 mi. NW Miami		

ILLINOIS

Perry Army Air Field	3 mi. S Perry	Chanute Field	1 mi. S Rantoul
Pinecastle Army Air Field	7 mi. SE Pinecastle	Chicago Municipal Airport	8 mi. SW Loop District
Pinellas Army Air Field	10 mi. N St. Petersburg	Curtiss-Steinberg	4 mi. SSW East St. Louis
Prospect Field (Boca Raton AAF, aux.)	1 mi. WNW Boca Raton	George Field	4 mi. NE Lawrenceville
Punta Gorda Army Air Field	4 mi. ESE Punta Gorda	Orchard Place Airport	14 mi. NW Chicago
Sarasota Army Air Field	4 mi. NNW Sarasota	Presbyterian Church aux. #3	4 mi. WNW Lawrenceville
Taylor Field	1 mi. SW Ocala	Scott Field	9 mi. NE Belleville
Tyndall Field	8 mi. SE Panama City	St. Charles Field	3 mi. E St. Charles
Venice Army Air Field	Venice		

INDIANA

| Zephyrhills Army Air Field | 1 mi. SE Zephyrhills | Atterbury Army Air Field | 3 mi. N Columbus |

GEORGIA

Adel Field	2 mi. W Adel	Baer Field	5 mi. SW Fort Wayne
Atlanta Municipal Airport	8 mi. S Atlanta	Bendix Field	3 mi. NW South Bend
		Emison (George Field, aux.)	4 mi. WSW Oaktown
		Evansville Municipal Airport	5 mi. NE Evansville
		Freeman Field	2 mi. S Seymour

Name of Field/Airstrip	Miles and Direction from Nearest City/Town
Madison Army Air Field	6 mi. NNW Madison
St. Anne (Freeman Field, aux.)	2 mi. NNE North Vernon
Stout Field	5 mi. SW Indianapolis
Walesboro Field (Freeman Field, aux.)	1 mi. WSW Walesboro

IOWA

Burlington Field	2 mi. SSW Burlington
Des Moines Field	3 mi. SSW Des Moines
Sioux City Army Air Base	6 mi. SSE Sioux City
Sioux Falls Army Air Base	3 mi. NE Sioux Falls

KANSAS

Atkinson Field	3 mi. NW Pittsburg
Coffeyville Army Air Field	5 mi. NNW Coffeyville
Coffeyville AAF aux. #3	16 mi. ENE Coffeyville
Coffeyville Field	2 mi. NW Coffeyville
Dodge City Army Air Field	5 mi. WNW Dodge City
Dodge City Field	3 mi. ENE Dodge City
Dodge City aux. #4	17 mi. NNE Dodge City
Fairfax Field	1 mi. N Kansas City
Garden City Army Air Field	9 mi. ESE Garden City
Garden City AAF aux. #1	19 mi. ESE Garden City
Garden City AAF aux. #2	13 mi. E Garden City
Garden City AAF aux. #3	6 mi. ENE Garden City
Great Bend Army Air Field	5 mi. W Great Bend
Herington Army Air Field	6 mi. E Herington
Independence Army Air Field	6 mi. SW Independence
Independence AAF aux. #9	12 mi. NE Independence
Liberal Army Air Field	2 mi. W Liberal
Marshall Field	2 mi. SE Fort Riley
Phillip Billard	4 mi. ENE Topeka
Pratt Army Air Field	5 mi. N Pratt
Sherman Field	1 mi. NNE Fort Leavenworth
Smoky Hill Army Air Field	5 mi. SW Salina
South Field aux. #5	4 mi. W Arkansas City
Strother Field	5 mi. SSW Winfield
Topeka Army Air Field	7 mi. S Topeka
Walker Army Air Field	1 mi. E Walker
Wichita Municipal Airport	5 mi. SE Wichita

KENTUCKY

Bowman Field	5 mi. E Louisville
Campbell Army Air Field	13 mi. NW Clarksville
Godman Field	Fort Knox
Lexington AFS	5 mi. W Lexington
Standiford Field	6 mi. SE Louisville
Paducah Municipal Airport (Nashville, aux.)	Paducah
Sturgis Army Air Field	1 mi. E Sturgis

LOUISIANA

Alexandria Army Air Field	6 mi. WNW Alexandria
Alvin Callender	8 mi. SSE New Orleans
Barksdale Field	6 mi. E Shreveport
DeRidder Army Air Base	3 mi. WSW DeRidder
Esler Field	10 mi. NE Alexandria
Hammond Army Air Field	3 mi. E Hammond
Harding Field	5 mi. N Baton Rouge
Lafayette Field	1 mi. SE Lafayette
Lake Charles Army Air Field	3 mi. ESE Lake Charles
Leesville Landing Strip	2 mi. NW Leesville
Mansfield Airfield	4 mi. NW Mansfield
Natchitoches Field	1 mi. SSW Natchitoches
New Orleans Army Air Base	6 mi. NE New Orleans
Pollock Army Air Base	4 mi. SW Pollock
Selman Field	2 mi. NW Monroe
Shreveport Field	2 mi. NNE Shreveport

MAINE

Deblois Flight Strip	2 mi. SE Deblois
Dow Field	2 mi. W Bangor
Houlton Army Air Field	2 mi. E Houlton
Pittsfield Field	1 mi. SSE Pittsfield
Presque Isle Army Air Field	2 mi. WNW Presque Isle

MARYLAND

Baltimore Army Air Field	6 mi. SE Baltimore
Edgewood Arsenal	1 mi. S Edgewood Arsenal
Fort Meade	Fort Meade
Martin Field (Baltimore AAF aux.)	10 mi. NE Baltimore
Phillips Field	5 mi. SE Aberdeen
Salisbury Airfield	1 mi. NE Salisbury
Salisbury Field #2	5 mi. ESE Salisbury

MASSACHUSETTS

Barnes Airport	3 mi. NNE Westfield
New Bedford Army Air Field	2 mi. SE Bedford
Boston Municipal Airport	4 mi. E Boston
Fort Devens Army Air Field	1 mi. NW Avers
Hyannis Airfield	1 mi. N Hyannis
New Bedford Army Air Field	2 mi. NW New Bedford
Otis Field	8 mi. NE Falmouth
Westover Field	4 mi. NE Chicopee

MICHIGAN

Alpena Army Air Field	7 mi. WNW Alpena
Detroit City Field	6 mi. NE Detroit
Grayling Army Air Field	1 mi. NW Grayling
Kalamazoo Field	4 mi. SSE Kalamazoo
Kellogg Field	3 mi. WSW Battle Creek
Kent County Field	4 mi. SSE Grand Rapids

NAME OF FIELD/AIRSTRIP	MILES AND DIRECTION FROM NEAREST CITY/TOWN	NAME OF FIELD/AIRSTRIP	MILES AND DIRECTION FROM NEAREST CITY/TOWN
Muskegon Field	5 mi. S Muskegon		
Oscoda Army Air Field	4 mi. NW Oscoda	Glasgow Army Air Field	3 mi. N Glasgow
Romulus Army Air Field	16 mi. SW Detroit	Gore Field	3 mi. WSW Great Falls
Selfridge Field	3 mi. E Mt. Clemens	Great Falls Army Air Field	4 mi. E Great Falls
Tri-City Army Air Field	10 mi. NW Saginaw	Helena Field	3 mi. ENE Helena
Willow Run Airport	3 mi. E Ypsilanti	Lewistown Army Air Field	1 mi. WSW Lewistown

MINNESOTA

NEBRASKA

Camp Ripley Field	7 mi. N Little Falls	Ainsworth Army Air Field	5 mi. W Ainsworth
Flyn Field (Glider Training)	12 mi. E St. Paul	Alliance Army Air Field	5 mi. SE Alliance
Minneapolis Field (Chamberlain)	6 mi. SSE Minneapolis	Bruning Army Air Field	8 mi. E Bruning
Rochester Municipal Airport	1 mi. SE Rochester	Fairmont Army Air Field	2 mi. S Fairmont
St. Paul Municipal Airport	2 mi. SE St. Paul	Grand Island Army Air Field	2 mi. NNE Grand Island
		Grand Island (aux.)	2 mi. NE Grand Island

MISSISSIPPI

		Harvard Army Air Field	2 mi. N Harvard
Hancock County Bombing Range	9 mi. NW Bay St. Louis	Kearney Army Air Field	1 mi. E Kearney
Columbus Army Air Field	10 mi. NNW Columbus	Lee Bird Field	3 mi. ESE North Platte
Greenville Army Air Field	8 mi. NE Greenville	Lincoln Army Air Field	7 mi. NW Lincoln
Greenville-Washington County Field	2 mi. E Greenville	McCook Army Air Field	7 mi. NNW McCook
Greenwood Army Air Field	6 mi. SE Greenwood	Offutt Field	9 mi. S Omaha
Greenwood Field	2 mi. SW Greenwood	Omaha Field	3 mi. NE Omaha
Grenada Army Air Field	4 mi. NE Grenada	Scottsbluff Army Air Field	3 mi. E Scottsbluff
Gulfport Army Air Field	3 mi. NE Gulfport	Scribner Army Air Field	2 mi. S Scribner
Gulfport Field	1 mi. N Gulfport	Union Field	5 mi. NNE Lincoln
Hancock County Airport	8 mi. NW Bay St. Louis		
Hinds County (Jackson AB aux.)	13 mi. W Jackson		

NEVADA

Hattiesburg Army Air Field	4 mi. SE Hattiesburg		
Jackson Air Base	3 mi. NW Jackson	Caliente Flight Strip	21 mi. W Caliente
Kessler Field	2 mi. W Biloxi	Camp Raleigh Field	2 mi. S Camp Raleigh
Key Field	3 mi. SW Meridian	Freeman Field	5 mi. SE Fallon
Laurel Army Air Field	3 mi. SW Laurel	Indian Springs Army Air Field	1 mi. N Indian Springs
Lime Prairie Field (Jackson		Lahontan Flight Strip	15 mi. S Fernley
AAB aux.)	30 mi. ENE Jackson	Las Vegas Army Air Field	7 mi. NE Las Vegas
		Las Vegas Airfield	6 mi. NE Las Vegas

MISSOURI

		Owyhee Flight Strip	4 mi. W Owyhee
Chester Field	4 mi. NW McBride	Reno Army Air Base	10 mi. NNW Reno
Columbia Field	2 mi. NW Columbia	Tonopah Army Air Field	8 mi. E Tonopah
Deblois Flight Strip	2 mi. S Deblois	Tonopah (aux. #5)	44 mi. SE Tonopah
Dexter AAF (aux. #1)	1 mi. SSE Dexter		
Fort Leonard Wood	SW corner		

NEW HAMPSHIRE

Gideon AAF (aux. #4)	1 mi. SE Gideon		
Jefferson Barracks	10 mi. SW St. Louis	Claremont Field	1 mi. W Claremont
Joplin Field	5 mi. NNE Joplin	Concord Field	1 mi. ENE Concord
Kansas City Municipal Airport	1 mi. N Kansas City	Grenier Field	4 mi. S Manchester
Lambert Field	11 mi. NW St. Louis	Nashua Field	3 mi. WNW Nashua
Malden Army Air Field	2 mi. NNW Malden	Portsmouth Airfield	3 mi. W Portsmouth
Rosecrans Field	4 mi. NW St. Joseph		
Sedalia Army Air Field	2 mi. S Knobnoster		

NEW JERSEY

Vichy Army Air Field	12 mi. W Rolla		
		Bendix Airport	Bendix

MONTANA

		Caldwell-Wright Field	2 mi. N Caldwell
		Fort Dix Army Air Base	1 mi. SW Wrightstown
Cut Bank Army Air Field	2 mi. SW Cut Bank	Milleville Army Air Field	3 mi. SW Milleville
Dell Flight Strip	1 mi. NW Dell	Moorestown Field	2 mi. NNE Moorestown
		Newark Army Air Field	2 mi. S Newark
		Fort Dix Army Air Base	1 mi. SE Wrightstown

NAME OF FIELD/AIRSTRIP	MILES AND DIRECTION FROM NEAREST CITY/TOWN	NAME OF FIELD/AIRSTRIP	MILES AND DIRECTION FROM NEAREST CITY/TOWN

NEW MEXICO

Alamogordo Army Air Field	9 mi. WSW Alamogordo
Albuquerque Army Air Field	3 mi. S Albuquerque
Camp Luna	7 mi. NW Las Vegas
Carlsbad Army Air Field	2 mi. S Carlsbad
Carlsbad AAF (aux. #1)	10 mi. S Carlsbad
Clovis Army Air Field	5 mi. W Clovis
Crews Field	12 mi. SSW Raton
Deming Army Air Field	2 mi. E Deming
Deming AAF (aux. #1)	19 mi. SSW Deming
Deming AAF (aux. #2)	11 mi. W Deming
Fort Sumner Army Air Field	1 mi. E Fort Sumner
Fort Sumner AAF (aux. #5)	16 mi. ENE Fort Sumner
Hobbs Army Air Field	4 mi. NW Hobbs
Kirkland Field	3 mi. SSE Albuquerque
Roswell Army Air Field	7 mi. S Roswell
Roswell AAF (aux. #1)	8 mi. SW Roswell
Santa Fe Army Air Field	10 mi. WSW Santa Fe

NEW YORK

Albany Field	7 mi. NNW Albany
Buffalo Municipal Airport	8 mi. ENE Buffalo
Elizabeth Field	West end of Fisher's Island
Farmingdale Army Air Field	1 mi. E Farmingdale
Idlewild Airfield	13 mi. SE New York
LaGuardia Field	5 mi. E New York
Mastic Flight Strip	2 mi. NW Mastic
Mitchel Field	1 mi. NE Hempstead
Montgomery Field (USMA aux. #1)	2 mi. SW Montgomery
New Hackensack (USMA aux. #3)	1 mi. W New Hackensack
Niagara Falls Field	4 mi. E Niagara Falls
Niagara Municipal Airport	6 mi. SW Niagara Falls
Rome Army Air Field	2 mi. ENE Rome
Rome Flight Strip	26 mi. S Rome
Roosevelt NAF	2 mi. ESE Mineola
Stewart Field	8 mi. NNW Newburgh
Suffolk County Army Air Field	1 mi. NE Westhampton Beach
Syracuse Army Air Base	4 mi. NNE Syracuse
Suffolk County	4 mi. N Westhampton Beach
Syracuse Field	6 mi. WNW Syracuse
Wallkill (UAMA aux. #2)	3 mi. NW Wallkill
Watertown Field	6 mi. NW Watertown
Wheeler-Sack Field	11 mi. ENE Watertown
Westchester County Airport	4 mi. NE White Plains

NORTH CAROLINA

Ashville-Hendersonville Field	12 mi. SSE Ashville
Barco Flight Strip	2 mi. W Barco
Bluethenthal Field	3 mi. NE Wilmington
Camp Davis Army Air Field	1 mi. NNE Hollyridge
Camp Mackall Field	4 mi. E Hoffman

Charlotte Municipal Field	6 mi. W Charlotte
Fairchild Aircraft Field	2 mi. E Burlington
Balloon Field (aux. #1)	1 mi. NNW Fort Bragg
Greensboro Municipal Airport	8 mi. W Greensboro
Lumberton Field #2 (Gliders)	3 mi. WSW Lumberton
Hoffman (Camp Mackall)	4 mi. NE Hoffman
Laurinburg-Maxton Army Air Base	2 mi. N Maxton
Morris Field	5 mi. WSW Charlotte
Pope Field	12 mi. NW Fayetteville
Raleigh Durham Army Air Field	11 mi. NW Raleigh Durham
Smith-Reynolds Airport	2 mi. N Winston-Salem
Seymour Johnson Field	3 mi. SE Goldsboro

NORTH DAKOTA

Bismarck Municipal Airport	2 mi. SE Bismarck
Fargo Municipal Airport	2 mi. NW Fargo

OHIO

Cleveland Municipal Airport	9 mi. SW Cleveland
Clinton County Army Air Field	1 mi. E Wilmington
Dayton Municipal Airport	12 mi. N Dayton
Lockbourne Army Air Field	9 mi. S Columbus
Lunken Airport	4 mi. E Cincinnati
Middletown Field	1 mi. N Middletown
Patterson Field	10 mi. SE Dayton
Toledo Field	7 mi. SSE Toledo
Wright Field	5 mi. E Dayton

OKLAHOMA

Altus Army Air Field	2 mi. ENE Altus
Ardmore Army Air Field	9 mi. N Ardmore
Bethany Field #2	8 mi. WNW Oklahoma City
Enid Army Air Field	5 mi. SSW Enid
Frederick Army Air Field	2 mi. SE Frederick
Gage Airfield (Will Rogers Field aux.)	2 mi. SSW Gage
Great Salt Plains Bombing Range	6 mi. NE Jet
Hobart Airfield	3 mi. SE Hobart
Miami Field	2 mi. NNW Miami
Muskogee Airport	2 mi. W Muskogee
Muskogee Army Air Field (Will Rogers Field S. B.)	5 mi. S Muskogee
Perry Airfield	6 mi. N Perry
Ponca City Field	3 mi. NNW Ponca City
Tinker Field	9 mi. SE Oklahoma City
Tulsa Field	6 mi. NE Tulsa
Tulsa AAF	7 mi. ENE Tulsa
Will Rogers Field	7 mi. SW Oklahoma City
Woodring Field	5 mi. ESE Enid
Woodward Army Air Field	7 mi. W Woodward

NAME OF FIELD/AIRSTRIP	MILES AND DIRECTION FROM NEAREST CITY/TOWN	NAME OF FIELD/AIRSTRIP	MILES AND DIRECTION FROM NEAREST CITY/TOWN
OREGON		Owens Field	3 mi. SE Columbia
Alkali Lake Flight Strip	14 mi. SW Wagontire	Shaw Field	7 mi. NW Sumter
Aurora Flight Strip	1 mi. NW Aurora	Spartanburg Airfield	2 mi. SSW Spartanburg
Boardman Bombing Range	3 mi. S Arlington	Walterboro Army Air Field	2 mi. NE Walterboro
Boardman Flight Strip	5 mi. WSW Boardman	Wampee Flight Strip	3 mi. S Wampee
Corvallis Army Air Field	2 mi. S Corvallis		
Eugene Municipal Airport	7 mi. NW Eugene	**SOUTH DAKOTA**	
Hillsboro Municipal Airport	2 mi. NE Hillsboro	Mitchell Army Air Field	4 mi. N Mitchell
Madris Army Air Field	2 mi. NNW Madris	Pierre Army Air Field	4 mi. ENE Pierre
Mahlon Sweet Field	8 mi. NW Eugene	Rapid City Army Air Base	9 mi. NE Rapid City
McMinnville Airfield	3 mi. ESE McMinnville	Sioux Falls Army Air Field	2 mi. NNW Sioux Falls
Medford Army Air Field	2 mi. N Medford	Watertown Army Air Field	2 mi. NW Watertown
Pendleton Field	3 mi. NW Pendleton		
Portland Army Air Base	6 mi. NNE Portland	**TENNESSEE**	
Redmond Army Air Field	1 mi. ESE Redmond	Berry Field	6 mi. SE Nashville
Rome Flight Strip	27 mi. SW Rome	Dyersburg Army Air Field	12 mi. S Dyersburg
Salem Army Air Field	1 mi. SE Salem	McKeller Field	5 mi. W Jackson
The Dalles Field	2 mi. NE The Dalles	Memphis Municipal Airport	8 mi. SE Memphis
		Smyrna Army Air Field	1 mi. N Smyrna
PENNSYLVANIA		Tri-City Field	12 mi. NNW Tri-City
Connellsville Municipal Airport	5 mi. SW Connellsville	Wm. Nothern Field	2 mi. NW Tullahoma
Harrisburg Municipal Airport	4 mi. S Harrisburg		
Olmstead Field	1 mi. W Middletown	**TEXAS**	
Philadelphia Municipal Airport	6 mi. SW Philadelphia	Abernathy Field	6 mi. E Abernathy
Pittsburg-Allegheny County Airport	7 mi. SE Pittsburgh	Abilene Air Terminal	3 mi. ESE Abilene
Reading Army Air Field	3 mi. NW Reading	Abilene Army Air Field	7 mi. WSW Abilene
Waynesboro Municipal Airport	3 mi. SE Waynesboro	Alamo Field	7 mi. NNE San Antonio
Williamsport Field	4 mi. E Williamsport	Aloe Army Air Field	4 mi. WSW Victoria
		Aloe AAF (aux. #10)	20 mi. WSW Victoria
RHODE ISLAND		Amarillo Army Air Field	9 mi. ENE Amarillo
Hillsgrove Army Air Field	5 mi. S Providence	Amarillo Field	6 mi. ENE Amarillo
		Avenger Field	4 mi. W Sweetwater
SOUTH CAROLINA		Bergstrom Field	8 mi. E Austin
Aiken Army Air Field	7 mi. NNE Aiken	Biggs Field	8 mi. NE El Paso
Anderson Airfield (Greenville AAB aux.)	3 mi. W Anderson	Big Spring Army Air Field	3 mi. W Big Spring
Barnwell Airfield (Columbia AAB aux.)	2 mi. NW Barnwell	Big Spring Army Glider School	18 mi. NNW Big Spring
Charlestown Army Air Field	10 mi. NW Charlestown	Biggs Field	6 mi. NE El Paso
Chester Airfield	6 mi. NNE Chester	Blackland Army Air Field	4 mi. NW Waco
Columbia Army Air Base	6 mi. SW Columbia	Brooks Field	3 mi. SSE San Antonio
Congaree Army Air Field	15 mi. ESE Columbia	Brownsville Municipal Airport	5 mi. E Brownsville
Coranca Army Air Field	4 mi. N Greenwood	Brownwood Army Air Field	5 mi. NNE Brownwood
Florence Army Air Field	2 mi. ESE Florence	Bryan Army Air Field	5 mi. SW Bryan
Greenville Army Air Base	7 mi. SSE Greenville	Childress Army Air Field	3 mi. W Childress
Greenville Municipal Airport	3 mi. E Greenville	Cox Field	6 mi. ESE Paris
Hartsfield Airfield (Greenville AAB aux.)	3 mi. N Hartsfield	Dalhart Army Air Field	3 mi. SSW Dalhart
Johns Island Airfield (Columbia AAB aux.)	7 mi. SSW Charlestown	Dalhart Sub Base #1	10 mi. W Dalhart
Myrtle Beach Army Air Field	3 mi. WSW Myrtle Beach	Dalhart Sub Base #2	11 mi. NE Dalhart
North Airfield	1 mi. ESE North	Dyche Field	9 mi. SW Fort Stockton
Ocean Drive Flight Strip	3 mi. WSW Ocean Drive	Eagle Pass Army Air Field	10 mi. NE Eagle Pass
		Ellington Field	12 mi. SE Houston
		Ellington aux. #2	3 mi. WNW Houston
		El Paso Municipal Airport	5 mi. ENE El Paso
		Fort Worth Army Air Field	7 mi. WNW Fort Worth

NAME OF FIELD/AIRSTRIP	MILES AND DIRECTION FROM NEAREST CITY/TOWN
Foster Field	5 mi. NE Victoria
Foster aux. #4	13 mi. NNW Victoria
Gainsville Army Air Field	3 mi. WNW Gainsville
Galveston Army Air Field	5 mi. SW Galveston
Gaskin Field (Perrin Field aux.)	13 mi. SW Sherman
Gibbs Field	2 mi. NNW Fort Stockton
Goodfellow Field	3 mi. SE San Angelo
Harlingen Army Air Field	3 mi. NE Harlingen
Hensley Field	11 mi. NW Dallas
Hondo Army Air Field	1 mi. W Hondo
Houston Field	9 mi. SSE Houston
Idalou (aux. #2)	5 mi. ENE Idalou
Kelly Field	5 mi. SW San Antonio
Kelly Field (aux. #4)	5 mi. N Castroville
Laguna Madre (Sub Base-Harlingen)	Harlingen
Lamesa Field	8 mi. N Lamesa
Laredo Army Air Field	1 mi. NE Laredo
Laredo aux.	60 mi. NW Laredo
Laughlin Field	6 mi. E Del Rio
Louis Schreiner Field	4 mi. SE Kerrville
Love Field	6 mi. N Dallas
Lubbock Army Air Field	10 mi. SW Lubbock
Majors Field	5 mi. SSW Greenville
Majors (aux. #1)	11 mi. SW Greenville
Majors (aux. #3)	10 mi. NNE Greenville
Marfa Army Air Field	8 mi. ESE Marfa
Marfa Field	4 mi. N Marfa
Matagorda Island Bomb Range	8 mi. SW Port O'Connor
Midland Army Air Field	8 mi. WSW Midland
Midland Municipal Airport	3 mi. NNW Midland
Mineral Wells Field	3 mi. SE Mineral Wells
Moore Field	12 mi. NNW Mission
Moore aux. #1	10 mi. N Edinburg
Moore aux. #3	4 mi. N La Grulla
Palestine Field	5 mi. WNW Palestine
Palacios Army Air Field	3 mi. NW Palacios
Pampa Army Air Field	12 mi. E Pampa
Pecos Army Air Field	2 mi. S Pecos
Perrin Field	6 mi. NW Sherman
Pounds Field	6 mi. W Tyler
Pyote Field	1 mi. SW Pyote
Randolph Field	17 mi. NE San Antonio
San Angelo Army Air Field	8 mi. SSW San Angelo
San Antonio Field	7 mi. N San Antonio
San Marcos Army Air Field	3 mi. E San Marcos
Sheppard Field	6 mi. N Wichita Falls
Sherman Field	1 mi. NE Fort Leavenworth
South Plains Army Air Field	5 mi. N Lubbock
Stinson Field	6 mi. S San Antonio
Temple Army Air Field	6 mi. NW Temple
Terrell Field	2 mi. SSE Terrell
Waco Army Air Field	5 mi. NE Waco
Waco Field	3 mi. W Waco
Wink Field	4 mi. NW Wink

UTAH

NAME OF FIELD/AIRSTRIP	MILES AND DIRECTION FROM NEAREST CITY/TOWN
Dugway Field	45 mi. SW Tooele
Hill Field	9 mi. SW Ogden
Hinckley Field	5 mi. W Ogden
Logan-Cache County Field	4 mi. NNW Logan
Low Flight Strip	3 mi. N Knolls
Salt Lake City Army Air Base	4 mi. W Salt Lake City
Salt Lake Field #2	11 mi. SW Salt Lake City
Wendover Field	1 mi. S Wendover

VIRGINIA

Blackstone Army Air Field	2 mi. ESE Blackstone
Langley Field	3 mi. W Hampton
Melfa Flight Strip	1 mi. SW Melfa
Norfolk Army Air Field	5 mi. NE Norfolk
Petersburg Field	6 mi. WSW Petersburg
Richmond Army Air Base	6 mi. SE Richmond
Tappahannock Flight Strip	1 mi. SW Tappahannock
West Point Field	2 mi. ESE West Point
Woordum	4 mi. NNW Roanoke

WASHINGTON

Arlington NAAS	3 mi. SW Arlington
Bellingham Army Air Field	3 mi. NW Bellingham
Boeing Field	5 mi. S Seattle
Ellensburg Army Air Field	2 mi. N Ellensburg
Ephrata Army Air Base	1 mi. SE Ephrata
Felts Field	5 mi. NE Spokane
Fort George Wright	5 mi. NW Spokane
Geiger Field	6 mi. SW Spokane
Gray Field	1 mi. SE Fort Lewis
Kitsap County Airport	8 mi. SW Bremerton
McChord Field	9 mi. S Tacoma
Moses Lake Army Air Field	6 mi. NW Moses Lake
Mt. Vernon Navy Airport	6 mi. NW Mt. Vernon
Olympia Army Air Field	4 mi. S Olympia
Omak Flight Strip	Omak
Paine Field	5 mi. SW Everett
Port Angeles Army Air Field	3 mi. W Port Angeles
Quillayute Navy Airport	1 mi. SW Quillayute
Shelton Navy Airport	2 mi. NW Shelton
South Bend Airfield	6 mi. WNW Willapa
Spokane Army Air Field	10 mi. WSW Spokane
Walla Walla Army Air Field	2 mi. NE Walla Walla
Yakima Airfield	Yakima

WISCONSIN

Billy Mitchell Field	3 mi. W Lake Michigan
Camp Williams Army Air Field	1 mi. N Camp Douglas
Camp McCoy	3 mi. E Camp McCoy
Tomah	15 mi. E Sparta
Truax Field	3 mi. NE Madison

NAME OF FIELD/AIRSTRIP	MILES AND DIRECTION FROM NEAREST CITY/TOWN
WYOMING	
Casper Army Air Field	6 mi. NNW Casper
Cheyenne Municipal Airport	2 mi. N Cheyenne

NAME OF FIELD/AIRSTRIP	MILES AND DIRECTION FROM NEAREST CITY/TOWN
WASHINGTON D. C.	
Bolling Field	3 mi. S D.C.
Camp Springs Army Air Field	11 mi. SE D.C.
Washington National Airport	3 mi. S D.C.

REFERENCES

······································

FOREWORD

The Official Guide to the Army Air Forces, Pocket Books Inc. NY, NY, 1944.

Schirmer, Robert F. Col. USAF (Ret). *AAC & AAF Civil Primary Flying Schools 19391945, Journal American Aviation Historical Society*, Spring 1991,

Craven, Wesley and Cate, James. *The Army Air Forces in World War II*, Vol. VI, Univ. of Chicago Press, Chicago, Ill., 1955.

CHAPTER I

Dunston, Patricia J. *Certain Lands Southeast of Ephrata*. Soap Lake, WA, 1993.

Riker, Dorothy. *The Hoosier Training Ground*. Bloomington: Indiana War History Commission, 1951, Vol III.

Wakeman Probe, Wakeman General Hospital, 11/22/1946. *The Evening Republican, The Columbus Herald, The Republic*, Columbus, Indiana, selected news articles, 1942–1945.

History of the United States Army Hospital, Headquarters U.S. Army Hospital, Camp Atterbury, Indiana, March 1954.

Hinds, James M, *The History of Camp Atterbury Indiana*, 1985.

Hammon, Stratton. *The Impact of World War II on a Citizen Soldier*, The Filson Club History Quarterly, Louisville Ky., Vol. 59, 1985

World War II Times, Indianapolis, Indiana

History of Atterbury Army Air Field, Air Force Historical Research Agency, Maxwell Air Force Base, Alabama.

Hiebert, David. *Bakalar Air Force Base History*. Hqds Air Force Reserve, Robins Air Force Base, Georgia, July, 1986.

Foner, Jack. *Blacks and the Military In American History.*

Bartholomew County Historical Society. Columbus, Indiana. Selected articles.

Angelucci, Enzo. *The Rand McNally Encyclopedia of Military Aircraft*. The Military Press, New York, N.Y., 1983.

War Department Corps Of Engineers Engineering Manual. Ft. Belvoir, Virginia, 1942.

Letters/Conversations: Mr. Stratton Hammon, Mr. Wendell Ross, Mr. Merton Wheeler.

CHAPTER II

World War II Installations. University of Oklahoma Press, 1972.

History of Coffeyville Army Air Field. Air Force Historical Research Agency, Maxwell Air Force Base, Alabama.

The Coffeyville Journal. Coffeyville, Kansas.

Air Currents. Base newspaper, Coffeyville Army Air Field, Coffeyville, Kansas.

Coffeyville at 100, 1869–1969, History & Centennial Celebration. Coffeyville at 100, Inc., Coffeyville Journal Press, 1969.

Kansas State Historical Society. John Lamberto.

Coffeyville Public Library. News articles via Cindy Powell.

Letters/Conversations: Mr. Siegmund Betz, Mr. Merle Campbell, Mr. Bob Ingmire, Messrs. Joe & Howard Funk, Ms. Lucille Heady, Mr. Bill Ironside, Mr. Erwin Kaiser, Mr. Tom O'Leary, Mr. Bob Marcellus, Mr. Jon Pevehouse, Mr. Drew Taylor, Mr. Jim Taylor, Mr. Eugene Woehl, Mr. Rufus Wysong.

CHAPTER III

Station History, Lockbourne Army Air Base. USAF Historical Research Center, Maxwell Field, Alabama.

Craven and Cate. *The Army Air Forces in World War II*. University of Chicago Press, Vol. VI, 1955.

Fahey, James C. *U. S. Army Aircraft, 1908–1946*. Ships and Aircraft, Falls Church Virginia, 1946.

Verges, Marianne. *On Silver Wings*. Ballantine Books, New York, N.Y. 1991.

Wings. Sentry Books Inc. Granada Hills, Calif. December, 1991.

Sandler, Stanley. *Segregated Skies*. Smithsonian Institution, Washington D. C., 1992.

The Columbus Dispatch. Columbus Ohio.

The Circleville Union Herald. Circleville, Ohio.

The Grove City Record. Grove City, Ohio.

Conversations/Correspondence: Mr. Dave Bellmore, Mr. Keith Conrad, Mr. Mel Eisaman Mr. Tom Foley, Mr. Mel Gerhold, Mr. Henry Jocz, Mr. John Planck, Mrs. Dawn Seymour.

CHAPTER IV

Station History, Fairmont Army Air Field. USAF Historical Research Center, Maxwell Field, Alabama.

Mauer, Mauer. *Air Force Combat Units of World War II*. U.S. Govt. Printing Office, Washington D.C., 1961.

Tibbets, P.W. *The Tibbets Story*. Stein and Day, New York, N.Y. 1981.

Nebraska State Historical Society. Lincoln, Nebraska.

Hastings Tribune. Hastings. Nebraska.

Nebraska Signal. Geneva, Fillmore County, Nebraska.

The Lincoln Star.

The Miligan Nebraska Review.

Olson, James C. *The History of Nebraska*.

Conversations/Correspondence: Mrs Dorthy Bunker, Mr. Jim Bunker, Mr. Don Eret, Mr. Tom Harker, Mr. Murray Holmes, Dr. Andrew Matthews, Gen. Paul Tibbets.

CHAPTER V

Brief History of Herington Army Air Field, 1942–1947. USAF, Historical Research Center, Maxwell AFB, Alabama.

Steele, T. L. *Liberators at Herington*. June, 1971.

Airpower. Sentry Books, Inc. Granada Hills, Calif. July, 1971.

Birdsall, S. *Sage of the Superfortress*. Doubleday & Co. Garden City, N.Y. 1980.

Anderton, *David A. Superfortress at War*. Charles Scribner's Sons. New York, N.Y., 1978.

Redding, R. and Yenne, B. *Boeing—Planemaker to the World*. Cresent Books. Bison Book Corp. Greenwich, CT. 1983.

Army Air Forces Installations Directory, Continental United States, USAF, Historical Research Center, Maxwell AFB, Alabama.

Jablonski, Edward. *Airwar*. Doubleday & Co. Inc., Garden City, N.Y., 1971.

Rust, K. C. *Battle of Kansas*. C.B.I. Roundup, June, 1987.

Out of the Past. Kansas Historical Quarterly. 1959. *Herington Times*, Special Edition, July 1987.

Mills, Mark. *And We'd Stand There and Wave*. College research paper, 1982.

The Windy Post. Base newspaper, Herington Army Air Field.

Tatge, Sharon. *TriCounty Historical Society*, 1987.

Conversations/Correspondence: Mr. and Mrs. Floyd Barnes, Mrs. Virginia Brunner, Mr. Quinton Burgess, Mr. Forrest Clark, Mr. Edwin Stoltz.

CHAPTER VI

Base Histories Baer Field, 1942–1947. USAF Historical Research Center, Maxwell Field, AL.

Army Air Force Installations, January 1946. USAF Historical Research Center, Maxwell Field, Alabama.

Mauer, Mauer. *Air Force Combat Units of World War II*. U.S. Government Printing Office, 1961.

Caiden, Martin. *Air Force*, Bramhall House, New York, N.Y.

Loening, Grover. *"Amphibian" The Story of The Loening BiPlane*. New York Graphic Society, LTD., 1961.

Jablonski, Edward. *Airwar*. Doubleday & Company, Garden City, N.Y., 1971

Freeman, R. and Allen, Ian. *B26 Marauder At War*.

Riker, Dorothy. *The Hoosier Training Ground*. Bloomington Indiana War History Commission, Vol. III, 1951.

Fort Wayne News Sentinel. 11/412/47.

Fort Wayne Journal Gazette. 8/451/47.

Baer Field Beacon. Base newspaper. 11/3/45.

Harnish, H. *Paul Baer Scrapbook*. Allen Co., Ft. Wayne Historical Society, 1968.

Fahey, J. C. *U.S. Army Aircraft: 1908–1946*. Ships and Aircraft, Falls Church, Virginia, 1946.

Official Guide to the Army Air Forces. Pocket Books Inc., New York, NY, 1944.

Ryan, Cornelius. *A Bridge Too Far*. Simon and Schuster, New York, NY, 1974.

Ryan, Cornelius. *The Longest Day*. Simon and Schuster, New York, NY, 1959.

Butler, Roxanne. Editor. *The Greater Fort Wayne Aviation Museum, 50th Anniversary Book*, T.I. Graphics and Communications, Inc. 1991.

Conversations/Correspondence: Mr. Tom Brewer, Mr. Horace Dimond, Mr. Loran Herrberg, Mr. Roger Myers, Mr. Jim Ross, Mr. Ed Shenk.

CHAPTER VII

Base History Freeman Field Air Technical Service Command, Seymour, Indiana 15 June 1945 to 1 January 1946. USAF Historical Research Center, Research Division, Maxwell AFB, Alabama.

Station History, Freeman Field, Seymour Indiana, USAF Historical Research Center, Research Division, Maxwell AFB, Alabama.

USAF Airport Directory Continental United States. Volume I, 1945.

US Department of Commerce, Bureau of Air Commerce. Description of Airports and Landing Fields in the United States. Airway Bulletin No. 2, Jan. 1, 1938.

Twingine Times, Base Newspaper, Freeman Field, Seymour, Indiana, 1943–1945.

Jane's All the Worlds Aircraft, Crown Publishers Inc., New York, NY.

Osterman, Louis. *Freeman Field and Seymour, The Home Front In Indiana*. 1986.

Conversations/Correspondence: Mr. and Mrs. Paul Cramer, Mr. Raphael Nolan, Mr. Martin Ross, Mr. John Sprenger, Mr. Dave Timbers, Mr. Ray White, Mrs. Chuck Yeager.

CHAPTER VIII

Riker, Dorothy. *The Hoosier Training Ground*. Bloomington, Indiana. Indiana War History Commission, Vol. III, 1951.

Devlin, Gerald M. *Silent Wings*. St. Martin's Press, New York, NY. 1985.

Janes Fighting Aircraft of World War II. Military Press. Crown Publishers Inc. New York, NY, 1989.

Stout Field History. USAF Historical Research Center, Maxwell AFB, Alabama.

Army Air Forces Installations Directory. October 1, 1945.

Indiana Book of Merit. Indiana Historical Collection. Fischer, Robert T. *History 113th Observation Squadron*. Indianapolis, Indiana.

The Indianapolis Star. Indianapolis, Indiana.

The Indianapolis News. Indianapolis, Indiana.

Conversations/Correspondence: Mr. Harry Blair, Mr. Paul Cramer, Mr. Robert Fischer, Mr. John Hicks, Mr. Robert Larch, Mr. Jerry Sowers.

CHAPTER IX

Pollard, A. W. *Hendricks Field . . . a look back*. Sebring, Florida, 1994.

Craven and Cate. *The Army Air Forces in World War II*. Univ. of Chicago Press, Vol. VI., 1955.

Fahey, James C. *U.S. Army Aircraft, 1908-1946*. Ships and Aircraft, Falls Church, Virginia, 1946.

Willmolt, H.P. *B-17 Flying Fortress*. Prentice Hall Inc., Englewood Cliffs, N.J., 1983

Four Years of Progress and Service — Hendricks Field. Sebring, Florida, City of Sebring, 1945.

The Highland County News

Station History, Hendricks Field 1942-1946. Office of Air Force History, Maxwell Field, Alabama.

Conversation/correspondence: Mr. Jim Green, Mr. Walt Pierce, Mr. Spizz Pollard, Mr. Bob Schott, and Mr. Bob Schultz.

CHAPTER X

Station History-Smyrna Army Air Field. U.S.A.F. Historical Research Center, Maxwell AFB, Alabama.

Brief History of Sewart Air Force Base, 1941-1958. U.S.A.F. Historical Division, 1958.

The Rutherford Courier. Murfreesboro, Tennessee. Selected articles, 1941-1946.

The Rutherford County Historical Society. Murfreesboro, Tennessee. Publication No. 12, Winter 1979.

Gann, Ernest K., *Fate Is The Hunter*. Simon & Schuster, New York, NY. 1961.

Conversations/Correspondence: Mr. Steve Fitzhugh.

CHAPTER XI

75 Year Pictorial History, Chanute Air Force Base, Rantoul, Illinois, Donald O. Weckhorst, 1992, Evangel Press, Nappanee, Indiana.

History of Chanute Air Force Base, author, date, unknown.

The material in this chapter is taken from the book, *75 Year Pictorial History, Chanute Air Force Base, Rantoul, Illinois* with the kind permission of the author, Mr. Donald Weckhorst.

CHAPTER XII

Certain Lands Southeast of Ephrata, Patricia J. Dunston, Soap Lake, Washington, 1993.

Ms. Dunston allowed the author to excerpt her book, *Certain Lands Southeast of Ephrata*, for this chapter. She also took the pictures showing the field as it is today. Her book is available by contacting her at, 95 Ridge Drive, Ephrata, WA 98823-1925.

APPENDIX—USAF AIRFIELDS

This information is taken from the *Army Air Forces Station List*, 4 November 1943 and the *U. S. Army and Navy Directory of Airfields (Continental United States)* February 1, 1944. The author attempted to list every significant field used in any capacity by the USAF during that period. Not listed are primary training fields, and many grass landing strips that had no significant use. Since the number of airfields and landing strips were constantly changing during the war (dependent upon training needs) some fields may have been deleted or not listed.

ABOUT THE AUTHOR

Lou Thole has written many aviation articles, most of which focus on World War II, USAAF training fields. He is a noted aviation historian, whose work has been published in newspapers and magazines including the *Friends Journal* (the publication of the Air Force Museum) and *FlyPast*. A recently retired sales manager, he holds a private pilot's license and a glider rating. He lives in Cincinnati, Ohio, with his wife, Jane. They are the parents of three children.